Understand Your Dreams

Understand Your Dreams
1001 Basic Dream Images
and
How to Interpret Them

Alice Anne Parker

H J KRAMER INC
Tiburon, California

H J Kramer Inc
P.O. Box 1082
Tiburon, CA 94920

Editor: Nancy Grimley Carleton
Cover Art: Jeanette Stobie
Cover Design: Spectra Media
Typesetting: Classic Typography
Book Production: Schuettge & Carleton
Manufactured in the United States of America
10 9 8 7 6 5 4 3

Library of Congress Cataloging-in-Publication Data:

Parker, Alice Anne, 1939–
    Understand your dreams : 1001 basic dream images and how to
interpret them / Alice Anne Parker.
    p.   cm.
    ISBN 0-915811-32-4 : $9.95
    1. Dreams.   2. Imagery (Psychology)   I. Title.
BF10814.P37   1991
135'.3—dc20   90–50862
                                                    CIP

With heartfelt thanks to:
Dr. Thomas Maughan
Jane Roberts
Eya Yellin
Alvan Perry Parker

To Our Readers
The books we publish are our
contribution to an emerging world based
on cooperation rather than on competition, on
affirmation of the human spirit rather than on self-
doubt, and on the certainty that all humanity is
connected. Our goal is to touch as many
lives as possible with a message
of hope for a better world.
Hal and Linda Kramer,
Publishers

. . . For true symbols have something illimitable about them. They are inexhaustible in their suggestive and instructive power. . . . The meanings have to be constantly reread, understood afresh. And it is anything but an orderly work – this affair of interpreting the always unpredicted and astonishing metamorphoses. No systematist who greatly valued his reputation would willingly throw himself open to the risk of the adventure. It must, therefore, remain to the reckless dilettante. Hence the following book.

Heinrich Zimmer,
The King and the Corpse,
edited by Joseph Campbell

Contents

Acknowledgments

Several years ago, my friend Bosco d'Bruzzi suggested that I write a book on dream images. Like most serious dream workers, I had a powerful aversion to the idea of a dream dictionary, even though I owned a collection of fascinating versions of nineteenth-century best-sellers, including *What Your Dream Meant* by Martini the Palmist.

Then one day as I was leafing through *Heal Your Body,* Louise Hay's invaluable handbook on the metaphysical sources for physical problems, I realized that a comparable book on dream images would be an effective tool for anyone interested in dreams. My friend Sara Halprin suggested that I offer "associations" for the images rather than "meanings," and the book was on its way.

I particularly want to thank Louise Hay for inspiring the design of this book, and for her visionary, yet matter-of-fact, guidance.

I am also indebted to Gabrielle Lusser Rico and Tony Buzan, who independently developed similar techniques of clustering, or arranging information in a pattern of circles, as I have done with dreams. Rico developed this process of nonlinear brainstorming as a means of stimulating creativity and coherence in student writers in the United States. At the same time, in

England, Tony Buzan used a process he called "mapping" as a way of accessing both sides of the brain while organizing a mass of information. I have long used Tony's mapping technique, as described in his book *Use Both Sides of Your Brain*, to play with ideas and organize workshop material, but it wasn't until I read Rico's *Writing the Natural Way* that I saw how useful the clustering process could be for recording dreams.

Each of us is honored by constant friends who support and encourage us through the disappointments that lead to our success. I am privileged to include in this category Tam Mossman, whose expert advice has contributed enormously to my confidence and growth as a writer. My dear friend LaUna Huffines gracefully led me to the perfect publishers, Hal and Linda Kramer. My daughter, April Severson, my husband, Henry Holthaus, and my allies, Freude Bartlett and Mary Kathryn Cope, receive my heartfelt thanks for their years of relentless confidence in my work. This book owes a vast, if unspecifiable, debt to the friendship of Mel Lee, Lana Sawyer, Owen Sawyer, Barbara Such, Peter Bloch, Mary Platt, Kathy Vinton, Herb Long, Harold Cope, Terence Stamp, Sheila Rainer, Pamela Norris, Peggy Donavan, and Herb Goodman. I am also grateful to the members of my Honolulu workshop in Interactive Dreaming, who gave me such useful feedback while I was developing the image catalogue. Thanks to Sandra Brockman, Mary Kathryn Cope, Nancy Crane, Bosco d'Bruzzi, Carla Hayashi, Henry Holthaus, Jan Kaeo, Luana Kuhns, Patricia Martin, Garrett Miyake, Karen Miyake, Georgia Putnam, Jessica Putnam, Doris Rarick,

Helen Schlapak, John Squires, and Margaret Stallings. My thanks also go to all of those who have so generously shared their dreams in my workshops, on "Dreamline," my radio show, and in the "Dreamline" newspaper column.

Part One
Remembering and Understanding Your Dreams

Dream Work

Over the past thirty-eight years, I've worked with thousands of dreams—my own as well as other people's. And after talking with scores of clients, I've concluded that there are three basic barriers to satisfying dream work.

The first barrier is obvious and all too familiar: *not being able to remember dreams in the first place.* If this is a problem for you, begin by writing down any dream—or dream fragment—that you remember, from any time in your life. Follow the basic steps for processing dreams that I will outline in the next few pages. The simple act of paying close attention to a dream, even one from your distant past, is often enough to stimulate a new pattern of increasing dream recall.

But what if you can't *ever* remember any dream? There is still hope! Instead of recording a dream, record one of your early memories as if it were a dream. Start by recalling a childhood memory—if possible, choose one that resonates with strong emotions—but even a dimly remembered early event will do. Just one or two images, plus the feelings associated with them, will give you plenty to work with. Then, by processing this memory using the basic techniques that follow, you can open a door to the fascinating (and sometimes very practical) messages waiting just across the threshold of your waking consciousness. In most cases, once you have given careful attention to a dream or dreamlike memory, you'll find yourself recalling dreams on a more regular basis.

Now for the second and most common barrier to dream work: *not being able to understand the dreams you do remember*. In this section, I'll be providing you with some basic tools for unfolding the many levels of meaning that most dreams offer you. The index in the second part of this book will give you a head start on making sense of even the most impenetrable dream symbols.

The third barrier to dream work may be the most serious of all: *most of us simply don't have enough time to record our dreams*. No matter how dedicated you are, the pressure of getting kids off to school, the interruption of morning phone calls, and all the demands of your daily rush are there to interfere. With even a few minutes of delay, vital details of a dream can simply evaporate. One of my clients complained of leaving her dream notebook on a corner dresser instead of conveniently close to her bed. By the time she crossed the room, it was too late—the entire dream had faded from her memory.

How can you hope to make sense of what you can no longer remember? Even if you catch your dreams and remember them well, you still need some effective— and *fast*—way of getting them down before they slip away. The following eight-step process will help you both remember *and* understand your dreams.

An Eight-Step Process for Understanding Your Dreams

Step 1: Record the Images of Your Dream.

Dreams often have a funny way of happening all at once. They don't occur in a linear, one-two-three sequence, as do events in waking life. Writing them down in narrative paragraphs not only takes too long, but it often violates the sense of the original dream in which events relate and interconnect in a much more circular, holistic, and organic form. So rather than write your dream down, try dropping dream images into an easy-to-draw pattern of circles.

This takes much less time than the usual way of writing out a dream one sentence at a time, and also allows you to relate dream events to each other in a more flowing and flexible form. Just drop the dream's main images into a pattern of circles and then let the information cook while you get on with your day. For each element, draw a circle large enough to express the importance of each image or event. Use one big circle to "enclose" a few words that describe the central action, perhaps with smaller surrounding circles to represent the sequence of events. Don't feel it's necessary to duplicate the perfect circles of the following patterns. Quickly sketch a rough circle and jot down the basic images. See Figure 1 for some examples of possible patterns.

4

Figure 1: Sample Patterns for Dream Circles

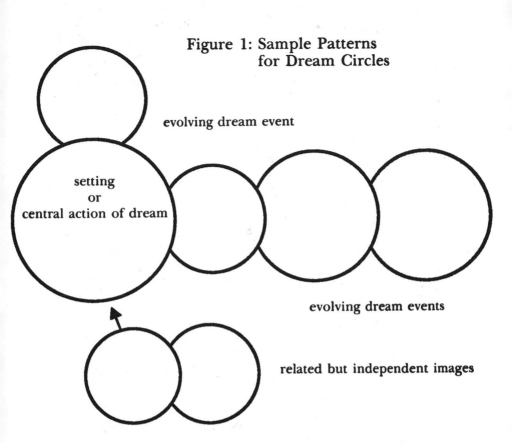

evolving dream event

setting
or
central action of dream

evolving dream events

related but independent images

You may wish to connect the circles with arrows or symbols.

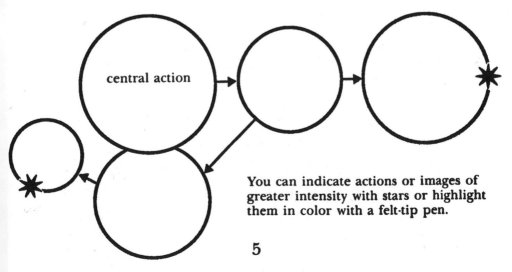

central action

You can indicate actions or images of greater intensity with stars or highlight them in color with a felt-tip pen.

With this technique, you can quickly record all of the dream's main components—more than enough to jog your memory later, when you have time to review the diagram. This method is not only faster than writing out a dream in complete sentences, but also gives you a more accurate record of the original experience. The "splash pattern" diagram allows you to relate dream events to one another in a more flowing and flexible form.

It may take a few mornings for you to become completely comfortable with this new system, but it will allow you to record even long and complex dreams quickly, even when you are particularly rushed.

Step 2: What Word or Phrase Best Expresses Your Feeling in This Dream?

You can tackle Step 2 as you are driving to work or sitting quietly with a second cup of coffee in the morning, or in the evening before you go to bed. Ask yourself, "How did I feel in my dream" or "How did the dream make me feel?"

The answer should be easy, if sometimes a bit ambiguous: "curious," "worried," and "confused" are common replies. With a bad dream, the answer may be "anxious," or even "terrified." An ecstatic dream may produce a "blissful" feeling; my own very favorite dreams leave me with a feeling that everything is just fine, that things are all coming together perfectly.

Often, though, the answer you give yourself will be a bit more complex, as in "I wonder why I haven't

6

lived in all these beautiful rooms!" Or "I can't figure out how to get my bags packed in time and I'm afraid I'll miss the flight!" Here, your clues lie in the emotionally evocative words: *"I wonder why I haven't lived . . . ,"* *"I can't figure out . . . ,"* and *"I'm afraid I'll miss . . ."*

Step 3: When is This Same Feeling Present in Your Waking Life?

Tracking down the source of each feeling can be a bit tricky, but in most cases you will feel an immediate tingle of recognition, and some particular area or issue in your life will leap into focus. Using the examples given under Step 2, you might discover that you haven't lived out your childhood dreams, that you can't figure out how to pack all the "baggage" of accumulated attitudes and beliefs and still "make the flight" to a greater awareness of what's really going on in your life.

By asking and answering these questions, you begin to use the valuable insight that every night's dreams offer you with such inventive guidance.

Step 4: What Were the Significant Activities in Your Dream?

List the key activities in your dream, and turn to Part Two. For each action, look up the associations given in the second column and the questions in the third column. If the associations and questions seem appropriate, write your answers down, especially if you've been dreaming about the same activities over a considerable period of time.

At first, some of these "typical" dream activities may be hard for you to pinpoint. Many of us have regular dream patterns that have become so familiar that we may take them completely for granted. For example, do you always find yourself hunting for a new apartment, fighting the enemy, going shopping, finding bills and coins, or trying to get a decent meal? I have been traveling in my dreams for my entire life. This activity seemed so natural and ordinary that I never examined the meaning behind it. Instead, I usually focused my attention on the method of traveling and the inevitable delays and problems en route, completely failing to notice that the essential framework of my dreams was so often a journey. It was a real breakthrough when I finally noticed that these dreams were giving me pithy bulletins on my personal *bildungsroman*, my inner search for the best routes and the most direct passage to my goal of greater consciousness. I continue to be on the road in many of my dreams, but now I'm more alert to the deeper meaning of these regular travel updates!

So consider the activities of your dream, particularly if they are familiar to you from many previous recurrent dreams. Look up these activities in Part Two of this book and see if the associations given seem appropriate to you. Sometimes these associations may not fit for you, but often just seeing what *isn't* perfectly accurate will stimulate you to come up with a more exact answer. Then ask yourself the question or questions that appear in the right-hand column. Again, even if these questions don't quite fit, they will usually give you a clue to the question you *do* need to ask.

Working With a Partner

Active dreaming is a lot more fun if you have someone you can use as a sounding board. Sometimes simply having someone else ask you the questions in the
right-hand column of Part Two will help stimulate an
answer. Sharing a dream dialogue with your partner
or mate, with other family members, or with a good
friend enriches everyone's dreams and the collective
awareness as well. Remember that increased consciousness is highly contagious.

Step 5: List the Characters in Your Dream. What Part of You Does Each Dream Figure Represent?

For Step 5, list the "cast" of your dream—the figures
and characters who appeared in it—and examine them
one by one. If they are real people known to you personally, they may represent themselves or your feelings
about them: your wife is really your wife, your friend your
friend, and so on. In unfolding the dream's meaning,
however, you will find it useful to describe these familiar persons with a word or two: "My wife is *capable* and
extravagant." "My friend is *weak willed* but *well intentioned.*"

Now, a slightly tougher assignment: ask what *aspects*
of yourself are reflected by these various dream figures.
In other words, in what ways are *you* being capable and
extravagant? How are *you* judging yourself as weak willed
but well intentioned? Also, look up Wife and Friend
to see what general associations those relationships may
present for you.

9

When apparent strangers play a part in your dream script, you can look up their roles or professions in Part Two. For Dentist, for example, the given association is "work on independence and power." If these associations feel appropriate to you, then ask the questions listed for each character; for Dentist, the question is "What part of me needs strengthening?"

Step 6: List the Significant Places, Objects, Colors, and Events in the Dream.

Once again, if the associations and questions listed feel relevant to your dream, write down your answer.

If your dream dentist in Step 5 was working on your teeth, you will find for Teeth the further associations of "independence, power, ability to nourish and communicate." Here, the questions to ask yourself are "Where in my life do I fear dependence?" and "What do I wish to say?"

List all the objects, places, colors, and events of your dream—especially ones that seem particularly vivid or noticeably unusual or out of place. In most dreams, certain places and objects will be prominent. When you remember the dream later, they will stand out with greater detail, or else you will sense a stronger emotional field around them. When you look up their associations and the questions to ask yourself, pay particular attention to these stronger images.

The associations given in Part Two are usually neutral or positive. If you dream about an angry dog, for example, you will find Dog associated with the positive qualities of loyalty and trustworthiness. If your dream dog seemed threatening to you, adjust the questions accordingly. Ask yourself, "Where do I feel *threatened* by lack of loyalty?" or "What do I *not* trust in myself?"

The list of images presented here cannot be exhaustive, of course. Anything you can imagine (and many things you haven't imagined!) will turn up in dreams. But, to track down the meanings and associations of these images, you can use related objects or ideas as clues. For example, if you dream that your teeth are falling out, you may be distressed to find that there is no listing for that exact image. But looking up both Teeth and Falling will lead you to the exciting questions "Where in my life do I fear dependence?" and "Where do I want to land?"

Perhaps, for you, fear of dependence has been a hurdle to intimate relationships, making you afraid to fall in love. Yet with this dream's help, you might discover that you really want to "land" in the kind of supportive and trusting relationship you have always longed for.

Personal Dream Vocabularies

Most of us have expanded dream vocabularies based on the interests and specialties of our waking life. In one of my dream workshops, an interior designer regularly reported dreams with richly detailed images featuring elaborate patterns and textures. To understand these dreams, she began by working with the

11

primary associations for images such as walls, carpet, furniture, chair, antiques, colors, and so on. To follow the more subtle levels of meaning, however, she had to take the further step of asking herself what she felt about each image's specific details.

One of the interior designer's dreams featured two chairs; the first she described as an original Louis XV side chair upholstered in lovat green silk jacquard. The chair was beautiful and valuable, but also stiff, fragile, and quite uncomfortable; this, she concluded, represented her discomfort with old principles and attitudes. The second chair, a copy from a later historical period, was less valuable, but much more useful.

She then considered each specific detail, seeking more personal levels of meaning. It was an education in style to hear her examine the precise significance of Louis XV versus Directoire, of lovat green versus viridian, of jacquard weave versus petit point. As she pursued each detail of these designs, more and more information unfolded about changes she was preparing to make—both professionally and personally.

When you work with rich imagery derived from your own areas of interest, ask yourself how you feel about the particular details in the dream that have caught your attention. Personal levels of association will quickly expand the general meanings and questions provided in Part Two of this book.

Sample Dream Analysis

Here's an example of steps 1 through 6, taken from my own dream journal. The dream story was brief, but

12

significant. First, let me report the dream in conventional linear form:

I am driving in a car with my old friend Joan. We are cutting class together to go swimming. I am feeling very pleased to have this time with her. Then I am leaving my daughter April at the train station. I feel a bit worried about her having all of the details of her journey together and making her connection to the boat on time.

I am uncertain which part of the dream happened first.

Using the circle technique of Step 1, I could easily and rapidly fit these two events or images into two large circles, thus:

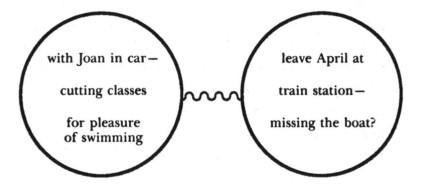

Since I wasn't sure which part of the dream happened first, I drew an odd wiggly line between the two circles. The activities seemed to offer different choices of behavior—as if one balanced, or excluded, the other.

Now for Step 2: What word or phrase best expresses your feeling in this dream? First I wrote the phrase "missing the boat!" That was my strongest feeling. I had awakened with the familiar sense of excitement,

13

coupled with that special anxiety that ship's whistles or train timetables can provoke in me. "Will we make it on time?" Then I also wrote: "*Worried* that I don't stay with April—but *pleased* to spend time with Joan."

Step 3: When is this same feeling present in your waking life? Ouch! No tingle of recognition for me. As soon as I thought about these emotions, the sensation was more like a nasty twinge in the back of my neck. "With regard to work and ambition," I wrote, "I am worried that I will miss the 'boat' of success—yet also, I believe that I already know what I need to know and that I can 'cut classes' to give time to old friends."

I noticed that in my journal I skipped Step 4, the question about identifying significant dream activities—but I'll return to that later. Now, Step 5: What part of you does each dream figure represent? I started by considering the characteristics of my daughter April, who was then a student at a prestigious university. She seemed to represent fulfillment of ambition to me. I also added that she knew how to enjoy herself and that I felt a deep and abiding love for her. Translating this information I saw that she embodied—or reflected—these traits for me.

For Joan, I wrote, "failure of ambition," "pleasure denying," and "betrayal of friendship." That is, I saw her as someone who had not fulfilled her early ambitions, who had denied herself many pleasures, and who had betrayed our friendship. I realized that she represented the part of me that feels like a failure, denies joy, and withholds love. Not a pretty picture!

14

After you have worked through the relevant associations and questions prompted by your dreams, you will have a good idea of what areas and issues in your life are clamoring for transformation. Now, instead of remaining the passive observer of events, you can become an active participant in your dream creation.

Step 7: What Changes, If Any, Would You Like to Make in This Dream?

Even a bad dream is a stimulus for change, pointing out where you are ready to grow. Simply because a bad dream *is* so powerful, it forcefully draws your attention to whatever area of your life is ready for work. A nightmare—about teeth falling out, for example— may be pointing the way to a joyous, committed partnership. Just recognizing that fact is a step in the right direction.

And, then, *decide what changes, if any, you would like to make in the dream.* Each and every element of your dream belongs to you. You can change it as you wish, and you will benefit directly and dramatically from the energy you release by doing so. It is almost always easier to make the change in a dream *before* you attempt a similar transformation in your waking life. Once you do so, you can trust that similar changes will begin to appear in your waking life.

Begin by imagining different endings to your dream, particularly if it is part of a pattern or series that has been cropping up again and again for any length of time. Rewriting your dream script is not mere wishful thinking. When you play around with alternative solutions, you are using what is sometimes called "lateral thinking" — creative, playful manipulation of the images generated by the deepest levels of your own consciousness to resolve what are often lifelong issues and limitations.

When you find a really satisfying solution to a long-time dream problem, review your new plan as you are falling to sleep. If, like me, you find yourself constantly traveling around, enduring the hassles of too-tight schedules and missing suitcases, then maybe it's time you chartered your own plane! In your imagination, declare that your flight will leave when *you* are ready, baggage and all, and not before. You'll even have time to go back for the red suitcase that fell out of the back of the car as you were racing to the airport.

Start by rerunning your dream in one of its familiar forms, but then graft the new ending in place. When you go to sleep, expect the dream to reappear with some surprising new twists, but now you are ready to resolve it with new solutions or a creative alternative — and be confident that you will wake up with a great feeling of success.

Going back to the previous example from my dream journal, I resolved to make a conscious change in that rather unsettling dream. What changes would I like to make in this dream? What parts of it did I enjoy? I wrote, "I would like to stay at the train station until April is aboard the train, thus guaranteeing that she will not miss the boat. I enjoyed the other part of the dream, knowing it was okay to take time away from

16

studies to swim and talk with Joan. I felt we could rebuild our lost friendship."

Changing Bad Dreams Into Good Ones

Several years ago, I worked with a woman who related a classic recurrent nightmare. In her dream, she would awaken to hear someone entering her house. All the appropriate creaks would sound, and she would hear slow, heavy footsteps coming down the hallway toward her bedroom. Frozen with terror, she would be unable to call to her roommates for help. As the door slowly swung open in the dream, she would awaken for real—to find herself in bed, trembling with fear.

In my client's first breakthrough with this dream, she found herself on a sailboat, watching her recurrent nightmare unfold on the screen of a television set. At first, she identified with the horror movie and was enormously frightened. But then, realizing that it was only a show on TV, she walked up to the set and changed the channel.

The dream had terrorized my client for years, and she dreaded its appearance. It was understandably difficult for her to approach it as an opportunity—to anticipate it and be ready to change it. I was very pleased to see her reverse this pattern: by watching the event take place on a TV screen, she was distancing herself from the fear and was genuinely prepared to "turn the old story off."

After this, however, my client experienced several very frightening dreams that escalated in terror. She also had a lurking fear that the dream was precognitive, warning of some event that would eventually take place in her waking life. The dream pattern escalated to incorporate this fear, so that she found herself waking into the dream, each time believing that it was actually happening.

My client regularly practiced visualizing different endings to the dream, replaying the new script until she felt at ease with a conclusion. All of her first solutions involved successfully calling out and having help actually arrive. In one early variation, it was a kitten who came to rescue her—that is, she was assisted by an aspect of the self that was feminine and cuddly, yet fiercely independent and able to care for itself. This solution made it clear that she was on her way to releasing and transforming the dream.

I have telescoped a longer sequence of dreams into these few examples. The process actually took place over a period of many months and included a number of variations on this basic theme. In the final stage of transformation, my client's dream reverted to its usual pattern. This time, as the door swung slowly open, she remained asleep and determined to see *what* was so frightening. It was a hairy monster. She looked at him carefully and concluded that he led a joyless life. Then she arose from her bed and invited him to waltz! The hairy monster was delighted to accept, and the bad dream melted away.

The invitation to dance seemed a brilliant resolution, and I was most impressed with my client's courageous struggle with her personal dream nemesis. She did say the hairy monster was not too light on his feet and annoyed her by stepping on her toes.

The general theme of this client's dream is actually a fairly common one. In her particular version, a hairy monster was the villain, although other clients of mine have encountered the frying pan man, the hot dog man, the balloon man, the homicidal maniac, and the Ku Klux Klan samurai. (The negative aspect of the self has many faces!)

Step 8: Briefly Summarize the Dream's Meaning. How Does This Apply to Your Waking Life?

In order to anchor and solidify successful dream transformations, it is useful to answer the question "How does this dream apply to my waking life today?" The energy released with dream resolution can trigger concurrent breakthroughs in waking life: perhaps a new relationship will blossom, or you'll find greater satisfaction in work. A successful pregnancy, or even the end of a troubling marriage can result.

In my dream of Joan and my daughter April, I asked myself that same question: "How does this apply to my waking life?" I wrote, "I'm afraid that I am taking time to deal with what is important but secondary, while denying myself the time to care for what is of deepest value for me. I fear that this pattern will make me miss the boat of fulfillment."

The last thing I did was to draw in my journal two new sets of circles. Into them, I dropped the constella-

tion of opposing traits that I observed in the two characters in my dream. The diagram looked like this:

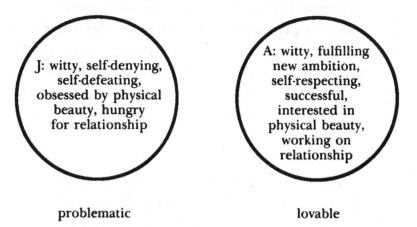

J: witty, self-denying, self-defeating, obsessed by physical beauty, hungry for relationship

A: witty, fulfilling new ambition, self-respecting, successful, interested in physical beauty, working on relationship

problematic   lovable

This step is an extension of the usual process. I
used it to understand better what parts of myself were
at issue in the dream. I then labeled one constellation
of traits "problematic" and the other one "lovable."

My efforts at changing this dream were followed
by a series of new dreams in which I was exploring and
evaluating new living spaces. Looking up Apartment
and House under images, I found the questions "What
part of myself do I occupy?" and "What do I believe or
fear about myself?"

Since Joan was often with me in my dreams, as I
considered whether the house or apartment would do,
I concluded that I was missing something about her that
continued to be important and that I was actively working on in myself. What might her greatest problem be?
The answer came immediately: Joan did not love or accept herself. This self-judgment she then projected to

20

the world at large, with a terrible effect on her relationships with others—including the men in her life, family, and friends like me.

I concluded that by exploring new living spaces with a self-judging aspect of myself, I was giving time and attention to a part of me that I had ignored and possibly denied. With this understanding, the figure of Joan disappeared from my dreams. April continues to be a regular member of my personal cast, usually appearing in dreams in which I am examining professional choices.

Finally I went back to the issue of dream activities, which I had so conveniently skipped when I was first working with the dream in my journal. I was "swimming" with Joan, but was afraid of "missing the boat" that April was heading for. Swimming is associated with freedom and joy of movement in the water—the area of the unconscious and of emotion.

A boat allows safe and rapid travel over water. I concluded that it was relatively easy for me to take the time to explore the unconscious joyously. For example, working with my own and others' dreams is a great pleasure for me! More pleasure than work, in fact.

However, I was concerned about "missing" a more conventional means of travel. Some of my fears about not being successful must reflect my reluctance to go places by orthodox means. This connected with my daughter April, who has decided to follow a conventional mode of success by returning to college. I reassured myself that I can always dive off the boat for a refreshing dip in the sea of dreams!

Case History Using the
Eight-Step Process

To review how to use the eight-step process for understanding your own dreams, I'd like to present a final case history: a vivid and meaningful dream experienced by a forty-three-year-old businessman who attended one of my Honolulu workshops in Interactive Dreaming. After processing the dream, he felt he achieved a significant personal breakthrough.

First I will quote his verbal report of the dream as he presented it during our workshop:

I am walking past the back door of my parents' house, where I grew up.

I look out the window, but see my reflection instead. I notice that I have an enormous erection and I'm nude. I look down at myself and see that I do have an erection, but it is nowhere near the size of the reflected penis.

I look back at the window thinking that it must be the type of glass that is making my penis look so big.

Now let me quote his written work on the dream as it appeared in his journal, with only minor editorial changes. His journal entry, using circles to diagram the dream, looked like this:

1. Record the images of your dream.

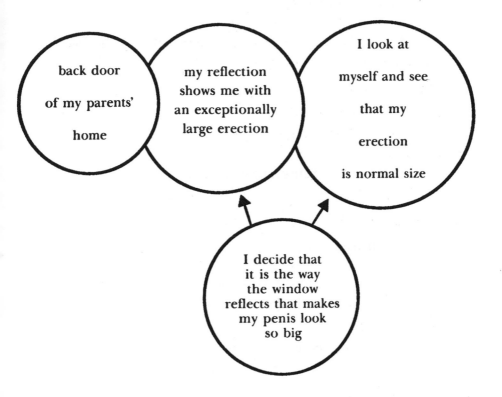

back door of my parents' home

my reflection shows me with an exceptionally large erection

I look at myself and see that my erection is normal size

I decide that it is the way the window reflects that makes my penis look so big

2. What word or phrase best expresses your feeling in this dream?

I am interested in the effect of looking bigger and more impressive produced by the back door window.

3. When is this same feeling present in your waking life?

In my awake life I have a similar feeling when the world perceives me as a successful businessman.

4. What were the significant activities in your dream?

I was observing myself, and, particularly, the "size" of my masculine attributes!

5. List the characters in your dream. What part of you does each dream figure represent?

Just me . . . representing me!

6. List the significant places, objects, colors, and events in the dream.

My parents' house = the parental attitudes, beliefs, fears, and also the beliefs I grew up with and still hold unconsciously.

My erection = creative power. What do I want to do or make? I do want to make a "big" success of my business. I want to feel as successful as the outside world believes me to be.

Nude = Where in my life am I ready to be seen? I am ready to see myself as successful.

Back = Unconscious, "back there," what I can't see. I don't consciously agree with my parents, but the fears and beliefs are still back there.

The back door is a passage out with a window that lets me view where it leads. I get a reflection as in a mirror, which makes me ask: What am I ready to see? I'm ready to see myself as successful, which would be a passage out of my parents' beliefs about limitations and success.

7. What changes, if any, would you like to make in this dream?

I would like to walk through the door and participate in the larger world's view of me.

8. Briefly summarize the dream's meaning. How does this apply to your waking life?

This dream is about the limitations of my beliefs, particularly unconscious beliefs about success in the world. As long as I continue to hold my parents' point of view, my power will remain relatively modest, even though the reflection from outside (that is, from the world) is much larger.

This dream didn't feel very sexual, although I think my parents' attitudes about being careful – not "exposing" yourself, never taking chances – also apply to sexuality.

As long as I am in my parents' house (of limited ideas, ambitions, and beliefs about personal power), I won't really own the power that the outside world already reflects as belonging to me.

In his dream, this businessman felt he had successfully "uncovered" feelings that had been limiting his *experience* of professional success, even though others saw him as already being successful.

Some weeks later, he reported another dream:

While preparing to make a journey that would lead to my death, I was looking over some treasured items that I intended to bequeath to family members.

As he worked with this extremely powerful dream, he concluded that the part of himself that was preparing to "die" was the outgrown self who had accepted his parents' fears. By bequeathing to younger family members the "treasures" he had accumulated, he hoped to leave behind a more expansive and secure vision than the one he had inherited. After processing this second dream, he believed that he had successfully transformed the old fears and reservations about success that had burdened his family for years, perhaps even for generations.

As this businessman discovered, actively engaging in dream transformation will increase your feeling of command over waking-life events. Instead of being the victim of circumstances, you become a creative participant — shaping inner and outer circumstances to fit your deepest wishes and desires.

Part Two
An Index of Basic Dream Images

Comments

All the items included in this index are organized alphabetically. But because it is often helpful to read over the associations for related items, there are several categories where, for easier reference, I have grouped together closely related images under subheadings. These categories include:

Animals, domestic
Animals, wild
Body parts
Clothing
Colors
Elements
House
Numbers
Sex
Vehicles
Water

All the items in these categories are also listed individually, in their proper alphabetical places.

For example, if your dream features the image of a dripping faucet, look up Water. You will find the subheading *dripping*, along with more information about the different meanings for water and emotion in dreams. These additional associations and questions will often help you relate that single dream to a much larger dream sequence.

Image:	Associations:	Ask Yourself:
Abandonment	Isolation. Leaving behind an old self. Release from control of the old self.	What part of me am I ready to leave behind?
Aborigine *See also* Native.	Intuitive self. Magical identity. Primitive wisdom.	Where in my life do I seek alignment with natural forces?
Abortion	Loss of the new. Failure to nurture.	What part of myself do I feel is too weak to survive?
Above	Higher self. Greater understanding or knowledge.	What do I aspire to? What do I want to know?
Abyss	Vast depth. Profundity. Infinity.	What lies deep within me?
Accident	Unexpected change. Upset.	Where am I avoiding change?

Acorn
See Seed.

Acting *or* actor — Role. Desire for recognition. — What role am I playing? Do I feel unrecognized?

Addict *or* addiction — Obsessive need. Lack of control. — What habit is a threat to me?

Adolescent — Lusty stage of development. Rapid growth. Immaturity. — What part of me is almost there? Where in my life is my growth most intense?

Adultery
See Extramarital sex; Sex.

African-American — Freedom from repression. — In what way am I ready to be more expressive and creative?

Age
See Young; Old.

Image:	Associations:	Ask Yourself:
Agreement	If good agreement, harmony or commitment. If bad, compromise.	What do I wish to resolve? What am I willing to settle?
AIDS *See also* Plague.	Hopelessness. Self-denial or guilt.	Am I ready to stop condemning myself and others?
Air *See also* Elements; Wind.	Breath. Intelligence. Force of mind.	What area of my life requires stimulation?
Airplane *See* Plane.		
Alcohol	Relaxation. Indulgence. Freedom from responsibility.	What do I want to release?
Alien *See also* UFO.	Distant, strange, or unrecognized. Nonhuman.	What part of me is strange or unconventional?

Alligator *See also* Animals, wild.	Primitive fear.	What elemental fears am I feeling?
Altar	Holiness. Sacrifice.	What do I worship? Do I want to give something up?
Ambulance	Rescue. Swift response.	What part of myself wants to save or be saved?
Anal sex *See also* Sex.	Submission. Union without issue.	To what or to whom do I want or fear to yield?
Angel	Transcendent knowledge. Compassion. Higher consciousness. Revelation.	What inspiration am I ready to receive?
Animals, domestic *See also* *subheadings.*	The natural self tamed by civilizing values.	What part of me is ready to be tamed? Or wishes it were not so domesticated?

Image:	Associations:	Ask Yourself:
—*camel*	Ship of the desert. Endurance.	What emotional resources am I conserving?
—*cat*	A feminine aspect. Cuddly and soft. Also independent and able to care for itself.	How am I integrating the yielding and independent parts of my nature? How do I feel about these qualities combined in a woman?
—*cow*	Docile and productive. Nurturing, if passive, aspect of self.	Am I passive? What do I nurture?
—*dog*	Usually a masculine aspect. Unconditional love. Obedient, loyal, trustworthy.	Am I trustworthy? What do I love unconditionally?
—*donkey*	Simplicity. Sturdiness.	Where in my life can I express my strength more directly?

—*goat*	Lusty vigor. Relentless energy. Omnivorous.	What am I determined to do?
—*goose*	Silly. Aggressive. Watchful.	Am I silly? Where in my life is my aggression apt to break out?
—*horse* See also Vehicles.	Swift. Usually elegant. Feeling of developed consciousness. Sometimes unexpressed sexuality.	How do I feel about my power? What natural force am I suppressing or expressing?
—*horse, flying or winged*	Soaring consciousness. Limitless nature of self.	What part of me is ready to soar?
—*mule*	Obstinate. Intractable. Stamina.	Where in my life am I ready to persevere?
—*pig*	Greedy. Smart. Sometimes slovenly, sometimes fastidious.	Am I grabbing more than I need or can use? Did I clean up my own mess?

Image:	Associations:	Ask Yourself:
—*rabbit*	Fertility. Luck. Insecurity.	Where in my life am I ready to be productive?
—*sheep*	Conformity.	What am I following?
—*talking animal*	Magical communication. Natural wisdom.	What part of my nature has a message for me?
—*toy animal*	Playful relationship with the natural world. Freedom from responsibility.	Where do I want more pleasure in my life?
Animals, wild *See also* *subheadings.*	Natural, untamed self. Freedom from civilization.	What part of me seeks free expression?
—*alligator*	Primitive fear.	What elemental fears am I feeling?
—*ape*	Dexterity. Mischief. Humor.	What part of me is almost human?

—*bat*	Nocturnal. Eerie. Keenly sensitive.	What darkness am I ready to navigate or explore?
—*bear*	Possessive love.	How am I threatened by love?
—*coyote*	Trickster. Rogue. Thief.	What adventures do I seek?
—*crocodile*		
See Animals, wild: *alligator.*		
—*deer*	Gentle beauty. Timidity.	What part of me hunts for protection?
—*dinosaur*	Fantasy. The power of size.	What part of me wants to be larger?
—*dolphin*	Natural intelligence. Transcendent wisdom. Compassion. Playfulness.	What part of me is divinely wise and playful?

Image:	Associations:	Ask Yourself:
—dragon	Mastery of elements. Abundance. Matter and spirit combined.	In what ways am I ready to align the physical and spiritual aspects of my nature?
—elephant	Wisdom. Memory. The power of persistence.	Where does my wisdom lie?
—frog	Transformation.	What beauty lies within me?
—giraffe	Overview. Shy grace.	Where in my life am I ready to extend my vision?
—gorilla	Strength. Innocence. Rarity.	In what areas of my life am I ready to be strong and gentle?
—lion	Nobility. Strength. Pride.	Where does courage dwell in me?

—*lizard*	Cold-blooded. Reptilian.	**Where in my life am I ready to show more warmth?**
—*maggot* *See* Worm.		
—*monkey*	Dexterity. Mischief. Humor.	**What part of me is almost human?**
—*mouse*	Meek nature. Quiet. Minor problems. Inner feelings. Shyness.	**What small troubles are gnawing away at me?**
—*rabbit*	Fertility. Luck. Insecurity.	**Where in my life am I ready to be productive?**
—*rat*	Street smarts. Clever. Sneaky and untrustworthy.	**Where in my life do I fear betrayal? Can I trust myself?**
—*skunk*	Passive aggression.	**Where in my life do I feel the need to protect myself?**

Image:	Associations:	Ask Yourself:
—*snake*	Energy. The serpent power of kundalini. Sexuality.	What energy am I ready to express or understand?
—*squirrel*	Hoarding. Running in place.	Where in my life am I ready to feel more secure?
—*tiger*	Power. Wild beauty. Sexual force.	What is dangerous in me?
—*toad*	Infectuous ugliness.	How or why have I concealed my true beauty?
—*toy wild animal*	Playful relationship with what is wild. Trust.	In what areas of my life am I ready to trust?
—*turtle*	Protection. Perseverance.	Where in my life do I feel safe when I take my time?

—*whale*	Power of the unconscious. Truth and strength of inner being.	What great truth am I ready to accept?
—*wolf*	Instinct. Appetite. Threat. Loyalty.	What instincts are a threat to me? What are my instinctive loyalties?
—*yeti*	Man-beast. Legendary.	What part of my greater self is stalking me?
—*zoo animal*	Wildness under control.	What instincts do I want to observe or enjoy in safety?
Ankle *See also* Body parts.	Support. Direction.	Where am I going?
Antique	Age. Survival value.	What part of me improves with age?
Anus *See also* Body parts.	Elimination.	What do I want to get rid of?

Image:	Associations:	Ask Yourself:
Apartment *See also* House.	A part of the total house of self.	What part of myself do I occupy?
Ape *See also* Animals, wild.	Dexterity. Mischief. Humor.	What part of me is almost human?
Applause	Recognition. Acclaim.	Where am I ready to ac-knowledge myself or to seek acknowledgment?
Archeology	Rediscovery of the past.	What ancient knowledge do I want to recover?
Arm *See also* Body parts.	Strength. To be prepared.	What am I ready for or getting ready for? What am I ready to give or receive?
Arousal *See also* Sex.	Stimulation. Availability.	What do I want to respond to?

Arrest

Enforced stop. Being caught.

Why do I fear being caught? What do I want to stop?

Arrow

Hitting the mark. Cupid's dart. Painful realization.

What is the point?

Art

Image of reality. Value. Creativity.

How do I express myself? What do I value?

Artist

Work on creativity and originality.

What part of me is ready for expression? Where am I unique?

Ashes

Remains.

What is over for me? What am I ready to discard?

Ass

See Animals, domestic: *donkey, mule*; Buttocks.

Athlete

Work on physical energy. Strength. Skill. Honor.

What abilities do I want to develop or be recognized for?

Image:	Associations:	Ask Yourself:
Atom bomb	Destruction on a vast scale.	What am I ready to end? What do I fear is ending?
Attic *See also* House.	Higher consciousness. Memory. Stored-up past.	What is "up there" that I want—or fear—to explore?
Attorney	Advocacy. Resolution of conflict.	Where in my life do I need help? What issues am I ready to resolve?
Autumn *See* Fall.		
Avalanche	Sudden release, often of frozen feelings.	What old emotions are about to forcefully break away?
Axe	Powerful severing.	What am I ready to chop away?

Baby	Infant self. Rebirth. Trust.	What is being born or reborn in me? What do I trust?
Back *See also* Body parts.	Unconscious. "Back there."	What is going on that I can't see?
Baggage *See also* Luggage.	Opinions. Attitudes. Material goods and responsibilities.	What am I carrying with me? How do I feel about the load?
Bag lady *See also* Bum.	Insecurity. Failure. Loss of identity.	In what way is my identity or success threatened?
Bald *See also* Hair.	Sexual issues. Wisdom.	What do I want to give up, or fear to lose?
Ball	Integration. Wholeness.	What parts of my being am I uniting?

Image:	Associations:	Ask Yourself:
Ball game *See also* **Sports.**	Integration of individual and collective consciousness. Wholesome competition.	What do I want to be a part of? What group am I aligning myself with?
Bandage	Protection. Desire for healing.	What part of me am I ready to heal or take care of?
Band-Aid *See* **Bandage.**		
Bar *See also* **Tavern.**	Relaxation. Indulgence. Irresponsibility. Pleasure.	Where in my life do I feel overloaded or stressed out?
Baseball *See* **Ball game; Sports.**		
Basement *See also* **House.**	Below. The unconscious.	What part of my unconscious is ready to be seen?

Basketball
See Ball game; Sports.

Bat
See also Animals, wild.

Nocturnal. Eerie. Keenly sensitive.

What darkness am I ready to navigate?

Bath *or* **bathing**

Cleansing. Release.

What do I want to wash away?

Bathroom
See also House.

Place of cleansing and release.

What am I ready to let go of?

Battle
See also War.

Conflict. Struggle.

What parts of me are at war?

Beach

Where conscious and unconscious meet.

What am I ready to be conscious of?

Bear
See also Animals, wild.

Possessive love.

How am I threatened by love?

Image:	Associations:	Ask Yourself:
Beard	Authority. Power. Wisdom.	How do I express power? How is my authority shown?
Beatnik	Rejection of social values. Isolation.	In what respect am I willing to stand alone?
Bed	Sleep. Rest. Retreat from activity. Foundation.	What do I wish to retreat or rest from?
Bedroom *See also* House.	Privacy. Rest. Intimacy.	What is my inner reality?
Bee	Activity. Productivity. Social life.	Where in my life do I get a buzz?
Beef *See* Meat.		
Beige *See also* Colors.	Neutrality. Detachment. Absence of communication. Status.	What am I ready to take more seriously, or be less serious about?

Bell — Signal. Recognition. Celebration. — What do I want to hear or fear to hear?

Belt
See also Clothing. — Holding up. Securing. Linking. — What am I ready to connect?

Bestiality
See also Sex. — Union with animal passions or instinct. — What basic aspects of myself do I fear or deny?

Bicycle
See also Vehicles. — Self-propulsion. Recreation. — Do I have enough strength to make it? Will it be fun?

Big — Larger than usual. Inflated. Generous. — Where in my life am I ready to expand? Where do I fear overexpansion?

Bigfoot
See Yeti.

Bill — Payment due. — What has to be paid for?

Image:	Associations:	Ask Yourself:
Billfold *See also* Clothing.	Masculine security. Resources. Identity.	What feelings about security am I ready to change?
Bird	Freedom. Escape. Liberation from weight of physical plane.	What part of me wants to fly?
Birth *See* Baby.		
Black *See also* Colors.	Isolation. Boundary. Separation. Introspection. Transition color.	What am I separating myself from?
Black person *See* African-American.		
Blind	Unseeing. Unaware.	What am I ready to see or to comprehend?
Blood	Essence. Life energy. Threat to life.	Where in my life is my vitality spilling out?

Blouse
See also Clothing.

Upper, as opposed to lower, self. Emotions.

What feelings do I consider appropriate?

Blue
See also Colors.

Harmony. Spirituality. Inner peace. Devotion.

What is the source of my peace?

Blue jeans
See also Clothing.

Community. Comfort. Freedom.

Where in my life am I at ease? Where do I want to be more at ease?

Boat
See also Vehicle.

Movement across the depths of feeling.

What emotions can I safely navigate?

Body parts
See also subheadings.

External form of internal nature.

What part is important?

—*ankle*

Support. Direction.

Where am I going?

—*anus*

Elimination.

What do I want to get rid of?

Image:	Associations:	Ask Yourself:
—*arm*	Strength. To be prepared.	What am I ready for or getting ready for? What am I ready to give or receive?
—*back*	Unconscious. "Back there."	What is going on that I can't see?
—*brain*	Intellect. Mind. Reason.	What am I ready to understand?
—*breast*	Nurturing. Female sexuality. Maternal love.	What am I nurturing? What part of me needs to be loved?
—*buttocks*	Humility. Stupidity. Power.	Am I being an ass? What do I need to forgive in myself?

—chest See also **Body parts:** *heart, lungs.*	Fullness of life. Generosity.	What do I want to experience fully?
—ear	Receptivity.	What am I open to? What am I ready to hear?
—eye	Vision. Consciousness. Clarity.	What am I aware of? How do I see the world?
—face	Identity. Ego. Self-image.	How do I appear?
—finger	Sensitivity. Awareness.	What am I touching?
—foot	Grounding. Direction. Basic beliefs.	Where am I going?
—hair	Protection. Attraction. Sensuality.	What am I covering? What do I display?
—hand	Capacity. Competence. Help.	What am I ready to handle?

Image:	Associations:	Ask Yourself:
—head	Intellect. Understanding. Superior.	What am I ready to understand?
—heart	Love. Security.	Where in my life am I ready to give and receive love?
—jaw	Will. Relentless anger.	Where in my life must I dominate? Where am I ready to yield?
—knee	Flexibility. Humility.	Where in my life do I need to bend?
—leg	Support. Movement.	What supports me? Am I getting somewhere?
—lungs	Breath of life. Freedom.	In what ways is my life ready to expand?

—*mouth*	Nourishment. New attitudes.	What am I ready to take in? What am I ready to express?
—*muscles*	Power. Strength.	In what aspects of my life am I ready to be more powerful?
—*neck*	Flexibility, especially of vision.	What can I see if I make a small adjustment?
—*nose*	Instinctive knowledge.	How does it smell to me? What do I know without knowing?
—*penis*	Male sexuality. Yang power.	How is my power expressed?
—*scalp* See Body parts: *skin, hair.*		
—*shoulders*	Strength or burdens.	What am I ready to carry? What is too heavy for me?

Image:	Associations:	Ask Yourself:
—*skin*	Surface of the self. Sensitivity. Connection between inner and outer.	What is on the surface?
—*spine*	Support. Responsibility.	What holds me up?
—*stomach*	Digestion of information or circumstances. Understanding.	What value can I receive from my experience?
—*teeth*	Independence. Power. Ability to nourish and communicate.	Where in my life do I fear dependence? What do I wish to say?
—*testicles*	Yang power. Masculinity.	What power am I ready to express?
—*thigh*	Power of movement.	Am I strong enough to get where I want to go?
—*throat*	Communication. Creativity. Trust.	What am I ready to hear and say?
—*toe*	Beginning, especially of movement.	Where am I preparing to go?

—*tongue*	The pleasure of taste.	What am I eager to try?
—*vagina*	Feminine sexuality. Yin receptivity.	What do I receive? What receives me?
Bomb	Explosive energy.	What is ready to explode?
Bondage	Restriction. Forceful limitation.	What am I afraid I might do?
Bone	Structure. Evidence. Support.	What supports me? Where do I look for support?
Book	Information. Guidance. Record keeping.	What am I trying to find out? Where am I looking?
Bookstore	Current information. Available knowledge.	What information am I shopping around for?

Image:	Associations:	Ask Yourself:
Boots *See also* Clothing.	Power of movement. Vigor.	What form of power do I seek?
Border	Where two states, attitudes, or life patterns meet.	What new area am I preparing to cross into?
Boss	Power. Direction. Control.	Where in my life am I ready or reluctant to take charge?
Boulder	Barrier. Obstruction. Building block.	What am I ready to surmount? How can I use the material that has blocked my path?
Boy	Yang power developing.	Where is power growing for me?
Boyfriend	Masculine ideal.	What do I admire in a man? What qualities am I ready to integrate?

Brakes	Control or slowing of movement.	Where in my life am I ready to feel more secure with my power?
See also Vehicles.		
Brain	Intellect. Mind. Reason.	What am I ready to understand?
See also Body parts.		
Bread	Sustenance. Shared resources.	What do I have? What can I share?
Breaking	Destruction. Forceful change.	What patterns or forms have I outgrown?
Breast	Nurturing. Female sexuality. Maternal love.	What am I nurturing? What part of me needs to be loved?
See also Body parts.		
Bride	Feminine receptivity.	What am I ready to receive?
Bridge	Connection. Overcoming problems.	What am I ready to cross?

Image:	Associations:	Ask Yourself:
Briefcase	Attitudes and beliefs about work and business. Professional identity.	How does my work fulfill or limit me?
Brother	Masculine aspect of self. Fellowship.	What do I admire or fear in myself?
Brown *See also* Colors.	Material world. Security.	What needs organization in my life?
Bubble	Soaring. Release. Unreal expectations.	Where in my life am I ready to rise? Do I fear my expectations will not be fulfilled?
Bug	Minor problems. Inconvenience.	What bugs me?
Bum *See also* Bag lady.	Failure. Outcast. Loss of control.	Where do I feel I am losing control of my life?
Burning	Consuming energy. Fiery release.	Where am I most passionate?

Bus
See also Vehicles.

Shared journey. Mass transit.

How does my personal power relate to mass consciousness?

Butterfly

Beauty. Freedom. Transformation.

What am I ready to change into?

Buttocks
See also Body parts.

Humility. Stupidity. Power.

Am I being an ass? What do I need to forgive in myself?

Cage

Imprisoning of dangerous elements.

What part of me must I control or limit? In what ways am I dangerous?

Cake

Celebration. Sometimes treat, sometimes indulgence.

Do I deserve a treat? Can I indulge myself?

Camel
See also Animals, domestic.

Ship of the desert. Endurance.

What emotional resources am I conserving?

Image:	Associations:	Ask Yourself:
Camera	Image of experience. Record. Sometimes a means of distancing.	How does it look to me? Do I want to be involved?
Camp fire *See also* Fire.	Companionship. Shared energy.	What companions do I seek?
Camping	Natural living. Back to basics.	Have I denied basic needs? Am I well grounded?
Cancer	Destructive growth.	What part of me is out of control?
Candle	Illumination. Search for vision.	What do I want to see?
Candy *See also* Sugar.	Small treats. Temptation.	Do I receive what is essential to me?
Cannibal	Part of the self sacrificed to the rest. Fear of integration.	What part of me is consuming?

Canyon	A channel in the flow of consciousness. Passageway.	What feelings flow through me?
Cape *See also* Clothing.	Dramatic protection. Fantasy.	What part am I playing?
Car *See also* Vehicles.	Personal power. Ego.	Can I get there? Who am I?
Carnival	Uninhibited fun. Freedom from restraint.	Where in my life do I want to cut loose?
Carpet	Protection. Insulation. Sometimes luxury or richness.	Where in my life am I ready to expand beyond my basic needs?
Car phone *See* Cellular phone; Car; Telephone.		
Castle *See also* House.	Fortified but noble self.	What walls am I ready to remove?

Image:	Associations:	Ask Yourself:
Castration *See also* Eunuch.	Denial of sexuality. Limitation of creative power.	What is threatening about my creativity or my sexuality?
Cat *See also* Animals, domestic.	A feminine aspect. Cuddly and soft. Also independent and able to care for itself.	How am I integrating the yielding and independent parts of my nature? How do I feel about these qualities combined in a woman?
Cave	Inner or hidden issues. Female sexuality. The past.	What is inside that I wish to explore?
Ceiling *See also* House.	Upper limits.	Where in my life am I ready to raise my limits?
Celebrity	Recognition. Fame. Sometimes notoriety.	What part of me wants to be recognized? Do I fear recognition?

Cellular phone	Accessible, expansive communication.	What communication is of vital importance to me?
Cemetery	Death. Transformation.	What is over for me?
Centaur *See also* Horse; Man.	Union of animal and human nature, or of instincts and consciousness.	Where in my life am I integrating natural wisdom with intellect? What aspect of my sexual nature am I healing?
Centipede	Poisonous feeling, thoughts, words.	What fears are restricting my progress?
Ceremony	Formal rite. Ritual.	What deep commitment am I ready to make?
Cesspool *See also* **Sewer.**	Accumulated negativity. Recycling.	What am I filtering out?

Image:	Associations:	Ask Yourself:
Chain	Bonds. The strength of many.	What restricts or strengthens me?
Chair	Position, style, or attitude.	What am I comfortable with?
Chalice	Inner wholeness. Spiritual self.	What spiritual thirst am I ready to quench?
Chandelier	Splendor of illumination.	What is my grand vision?
Channeling	Mediumship. Communication with higher realms.	What part of my greater self is ready to speak?
Charge card *See* Credit card.		
Chasing	Pursuit.	Where in my life do I deny my own power? What am I ready to catch?

Chasm
See Abyss.

Checkbook   Available resources. Convenient money.   What are my available means?

Cherub   Divine innocence. Angelic child.   Where is my spirit reborn?

Chest
See also
Body parts:
heart, lungs.   Fullness of life. Generosity.   What do I want to experience fully?

Chicken
See also
Animals,
domestic.   Scattered, disorganized thoughts. Small fears.   Where do I need to focus my awareness? Am I needlessly fearful?

Child *or* **children**   Innocence. The new self seeking to develop.   Where in my life am I developing? What part of my nature is childlike?

Image:	Associations:	Ask Yourself:
Chocolate	Gratification. Indulgence. Pleasure.	What do I want or fear to indulge in?
Choking	Restricted communication.	What am I afraid to say?
Christ *See also* Jesus.	Higher consciousness. Salvation.	What part of me is divine? How do I experience my own divinity?
Christmas	Celebration. Holiday spirit of festivity and light. Reunion.	What am I celebrating? What do I wish to reunite with?
Church	Spiritual belief. Organized religion.	What is the structure of my belief?
Cigarette *See also* Smoking.	Stimulation. Addiction.	What do I seek distraction from?

Circle	Whole. Repetition. Infinity.	What is complete?
Circus	Childlike joy. Fantasy. Profusion.	What do I want to enjoy?
City	Civilized order. Culture. Community or decay of systems.	How do my parts cooperate or fail to cooperate?
Clay	Receptive matter.	What am I ready to form or mold?
Cliff	Challenge. Precipitous height.	What do I aspire to?
Climbing	Aspiration. Growth with effort. Achievement.	What am I trying to reach?
Clinic	Detached attitude toward health and well-being.	What attachments are blocking my good health?
Cloak *See also* **Clothing.**	Magical protection. Secrecy.	What part of me is invisible?

Image:	Associations:	Ask Yourself:
Clock	Timing. Measurement.	How much time do I have? What is running out?
Closet	Storage of ideas or identity.	What is put away?
Clothing *See also subheadings.*	Identity. Self-image. Exploration of new roles or rejection of old.	What part of myself do I choose to show?
—belt	Holding up. Securing. Linking.	What am I ready to connect?
—billfold	Masculine security. Resources. Identity.	What feelings about security am I ready to change?
—blouse	Upper, as opposed to lower, self. Emotions.	What feelings do I consider appropriate?

—*blue jeans*	Community. Comfort. Freedom.	Where in my life am I at ease? Where do I want to be more at ease?
—*boots*	Power of movement. Vigor.	What form of power do I seek?
—*cape*	Dramatic protection. Fantasy.	What part am I playing?
—*cloak*	Magical protection. Secrecy.	What part of me is invisible?
—*coat*	Protection. Covering.	What am I covering up?
—*dress*	Self-image. Feminine self.	Who am I? How feminine am I?
—*handbag* See Clothing: *purse.*		
—*hat*	Opinions. Thoughts.	What thoughts or attitudes do I reveal?

Image:	Associations:	Ask Yourself:
—*helmet* *See also* Clothing: *hat.*	Protected opinions and attitudes.	What thoughts or opinions am I ready to change?
—*high heels*	Glamour. Restriction. Sexual invitation.	How comfortable am I with conventional femininity?
—*panties* *See Clothing: underwear.*		
—*nightgown* *See Clothing: dress;* Night.		
—*purse*	Feminine self. Sometimes sexual identity. Security.	What am I holding onto? What part of myself do I value?
—*shirt*	Upper, as opposed to lower, self. Emotions.	What feelings do I consider appropriate?

—shoes	General situation. Grounding.	How well do I connect with the world?
—shorts See Clothing: *underwear*.		
—skirt or trousers	Lower self. Passions.	What signals am I sending?
—underwear	Private self. Sexual identity.	What are my hidden feelings? What am I ready to expose?
—uniform	Conformity.	Where in my life do I wish to share with others? Where do I want to break free of rules?
Clouds	Transition. May be dark or light. Confusion.	What am I moving through?
Clown	Healing through laughter. Often bittersweet joy.	Must I suffer to be happy?

Image:	Associations:	Ask Yourself:
Coal	Unrefined matter. Source of heat. Potential diamonds.	What potential lies within me?
Coat *See also* Clothing.	Protection. Covering.	What am I covering up?
Cobra *See* Snake.		
Cocaine *See* Drugs.		
Coffee	Stimulation. Sometimes over-excitement.	Where in my life do I seek or fear arousal?
Coffin	Containing the end.	What am I ready to bury?
Cold	Emotional chill. Lack of circulation.	What warmth am I missing?

Colors
See subheadings.

—*beige* Neutrality. Detachment. Absence of communication. Status.

What am I ready to take more seriously, or be less serious about?

—*black* Isolation. Boundary. Separation. Introspection. Transition color.

What am I separating myself from?

—*blue* Harmony. Spirituality. Inner peace. Devotion.

What is the source of my inner peace?

—*brown* Material world. Security.

What needs organization in my life?

—*gray* Transition from one state to another. If clear, peace. If dull, fear.

What am I moving toward?

—*green* Growth. Serenity. Healing through growth.

Where in my life am I growing?

—*orange* Emotion. Stimulation. Healing.

What am I feeling?

Image:	Associations:	Ask Yourself:
—pink	Affection. Love.	To what am I responding?
—purple See Colors: violet.		
—red	Energy. Vigor. Passion.	What is my source of energy or strength?
—tan	Convention. Hard work. Propriety.	In what ways do I seek or avoid respectability?
—turquoise	Healing. Good luck. Protection.	Where in my life do I feel safe?
—violet	Spirituality. Boundary between visible and invisible realms. Aristocracy.	To what do I aspire?
—white	Purity. Clarity. Coldness.	What do I seek to purify?

—*yellow*	Vitality. Intellect. Clarity.	What do I wish to understand?
Comet	Messenger. Awakening or unleashing of energy.	What vision do I seek?
Commune	Collective energy. Socialization. Union of beliefs.	What do I wish to join? Who are my peers?
Companion *See* Friend.		
Compost	Fertile refuse.	What richness is buried in my past?
Computer	Facility of communication. High technology.	What area of communication is opening up for me?
Concentration camp	Fear and hatred of differences.	What is unique in me? What do I share with all others?

Image:	Associations:	Ask Yourself:
Condom	Sexual protection. Silliness.	Do I feel safe or silly about sex?
Convent	Spiritual community. Withdrawal from familial and worldly affairs.	What inner needs am I ready to nurture and support?
Convertible *See also* Vehicles.	Glamourous power. Parade.	What power am I ready to display?
Convulsions *See* Seizures.		
Cooking	Preparing to nourish.	What do I nourish in myself or others?
Cop *See* Police.		

Copier Repetition. Ease of reproduction. What message do I want to circulate?

Cottage Cozy, familiar house of the self. What part of me wants to be snug?
See also **House.**

Counselor
See **Attorney** *or* **Therapist.**

Countries Alternative realities or attitudes. Which of the qualities of this place do I find or seek in myself?
See also **Foreign.**

Country Natural world. Space. Basic needs and desires. Am I overcivilized? Do I feel confined by expectations?

Court Resolution of problems. Conflict. What issue am I ready to resolve? Where do I fear judgment?

Image:	Associations:	Ask Yourself:
Cow *See also* Animals, domestic.	Docile and productive. Nurturing, if passive, aspect of self.	Am I passive? What do I nurture?
Cowboy *or* cowgirl	Adventure. Romance. Independence.	What part of me wants to roam free?
Co-worker	Collaboration. Work on relationships.	How am I ready to be more cooperative? What is or isn't working for me?
Coyote *See also* Animals, wild.	Trickster. Rogue. Thief.	What adventure do I seek?
Crab	Soft meat, hard shell.	Am I too sensitive?
Crack	Possibility.	What opportunity am I ready to seize?

Crack
  See Drugs.

Crash
  See Wreck.

Crawling — Regressive movement. — In what areas of my life do I want to take my time?

Crazy — Total loss of control. Freedom from responsibility. — What holds me together? What happens if I lose it?

Credit card — Buy now, pay later. Ready access to resources. Protection. — What am I worth?

Creek
  See also Water. — The flow of feeling. — What feelings flow comfortably within me?

Cripple
  See also
  Handicapped. — Disabled. Limitation. — What am I ready to heal?

Image:	Associations:	Ask Yourself:
Crocodile *See* Alligator.		
Cross	Sacrifice. Suffering. Salvation.	What do I wish to transform?
Crossroad	Choice of direction.	Which way do I want to go?
Crowd	Throng of alternatives. Options.	What are my choices?
Crown	Majesty. To be chosen.	What part of me seeks acknowledgment?
Crying	Emotional release. Grief.	What emotions am I ready to express?
Crystal	Essential self. Clarity. Focus.	What is essential to me?
Cult	Unquestioning devotion. Sometimes obsessive beliefs.	Which of my beliefs are ready to expand? Which of my beliefs are limiting me?

Cup

Receptiveness.

What am I ready to receive?

Curtain

Protection. Decoration.

In what ways do I seek privacy? Or what do I wish to display?

Cut
See Wound.

Dancing

Joyous participation in life. Movement as transcendence.

What inspires me to go beyond my imagined limits?

Danger

Threatening change.

What am I afraid to lose if I change?

Dark

Mystery. The unknown and unformed. A place of fear—or of potential.

For what do I search? What seeks to take form?

Image:	Associations:	Ask Yourself:
Daughter	Youthful feminine self.	In what area of my life am I ready to express youthful receptivity?
Dawn	Beginning. Understanding.	What is beginning?
Death	End of a cycle.	What is over?
Deer *See also* Animals, wild.	Gentle beauty. Timidity.	What part of me hunts for protection?
Defecation *See also* Bathroom.	Elimination. Dumping, especially of garbage from the past.	What am I ready to get rid of?
Deformity	Misshapen. Disfigured.	What part of myself am I ready to accept and love?

Demon	Image of self-doubt or denial.	What stands between me and greater consciousness?
See also Devil; Monster.		
Dentist	Work on independence and power.	What part of me needs strengthening?
See also Teeth.		
Department store		
See Store.		
Desert	Isolation. Retreat. Endurance.	What do I wish to withdraw from?
Designer	Organization. Form.	What new plans am I ready to formulate?
Devil	Negative forces. Temptation.	What lies between me and my own greater consciousness?
See also Demon.		
Diamond	Purity. Clarity. Enduring treasure.	What is precious to me?
See also Jewel.		

Image:	Associations:	Ask Yourself:
Dictator	Control. Oppression.	In what ways can I be more flexible in making decisions?
Dining room *See also* Food; House.	The ritual of eating. Formality.	What sustenance do I require?
Dinosaur *See also* Animals, wild.	Fantasy. The power of size.	What part of me wants to be larger?
Dirt *See also* Earth.	If negative, unclean; if positive, fertility.	What do I need to clean up? What part of me wants to grow?
Disco *See* Dancing; Nightclub.		
Dismemberment	Pulling to pieces.	What must I pull apart in order to be together?

Doctor	Work on healing.	What part of me is ready to be healed?
Dog *See also* Animals, domestic.	Usually a masculine aspect. Unconditional love. Obedient, loyal, trustworthy.	Am I trustworthy? What do I love unconditionally?
Doll	Relationship practice.	In what areas of my life am I ready to be more caring?
Dolphin *See also* Animals, wild.	Natural intelligence. Transcendent wisdom. Compassion. Playfulness.	What part of me is divinely wise and playful?
Donkey *See also* Animals, domestic.	Simplicity. Sturdiness.	Where in my life can I express my strength more directly?

Image:	Associations:	Ask Yourself:
Door *See also* House.	Access. Movement from one area to another.	What space am I ready to enter or to keep private?
Dove	Peace. Resolution of conflict.	What problem am I ready to solve?
Down	Unconscious. Beneath.	What do I want to be aware of? What underlies my beliefs?
Dragon *See also* Animals, wild.	Mastery of elements. Abundance. Matter and spirit combined.	In what ways am I ready to align the physical and spiritual aspects of my nature?
Drapes *See* Curtain.		
Dreaming	Creating. Waking to inner reality.	What is real for me?

Dress
See also
Clothing.

Self-image. Feminine self.

Who am I? How feminine am I?

Dripping
See also Water.

Trickle of emotion.

What am I releasing, bit by bit?

Driving
See also
Traveling;
Vehicles.

Work on energy and power.

How far can I go? What is my desired destination?

Drowning

Going under emotionally.

In what areas of my life am I ready to feel more emotionally secure?

Drugs

Healing or making insensible.

What do I want to stifle or to intensify?

Drunk

Total insensibility.

Where in my life do I fear—or wish—to lose control?

Image:	Associations:	Ask Yourself:
Dump *See also* Garbage; Junkyard.	Refuse of living. Elimination.	What do I no longer need?
Dwarf	The power of the small. Unconscious forces.	What am I working to transform?
Dynamite	Explosive force. Sudden change.	What is ready to blow?
Eagle	Far-sighted vision and power.	What must I understand to be powerful?
Ear *See also* Body parts.	Receptivity.	What am I open to? What am I ready to hear?

Earth *See also* Elements.	Matter. Being grounded through nature.	How am I connected to the physical world?
Earthquake	Soul shaking. Deep levels of change.	What part of me is being shaken up?
East	Beginnings. Ancient truth.	Where am I heading?
Eating	Sustenance. Satisfaction. Pleasure.	What part of myself do I nurture?
Egg	Potential. Birth. Hopes. Wholeness.	What do I wish to develop?
Eight *See also* Numbers.	Eternity. Abundance. Power. Cosmic consciousness.	What am I willing to receive?
Electrician	Work on energy or life force.	What part of me needs a charge?
Electricity *See* Electrician.		

Image:	Associations:	Ask Yourself:
Elements *See subheadings.*		
—*air*	Breath. Intelligence. Force of mind.	What area of my life requires stimulation?
—*earth*	Matter. Being grounded through nature.	How am I connected to the physical world?
—*fire*	Spirit. Energy. Unpolluted and cleansing.	In what areas of my life do I seek to be inspired or renewed?
—*water*	Emotion. Dissolving. Yielding. Release. Cleansing.	What am I feeling?
Elephant *See also* Animals, wild.	Wisdom. Memory. The power of persistence.	Where does my wisdom lie?

Elevator	Ascension. Increased understanding.	What am I doing to get higher?
Eleven *See also* Numbers.	Inspiration. Revolution. Higher octave of two.	What am I ready to change?
Embryo *See* Fetus.		
Equator	Rite of passage. Movement from one sphere of activity to another.	How am I becoming more whole?
Erection *See also* Sex.	Creative power. Fertility.	What do I want to do or to make?
Eruption	Explosion of unconscious material.	What must I clear?
Escalator *See* Elevator.		
Eunuch *See also* Castration.	Cutting off sexuality.	How can I be safe and sexual?

Image:	Associations:	Ask Yourself:
Evergreen	Persistence in time. Unchanging.	What is eternal in me?
Exam *See* Test.		
Ex-boyfriend	Masculine ideal, either integrated or rejected.	What have I accepted or failed to accept within myself?
Excrement	Elimination. Garbage from the past.	What am I ready to forget?
Execute *See also* Judge.	Punishment. Judgment.	In what areas of my life am I ready to forgive myself?
Ex-girlfriend	Feminine ideal, either integrated or rejected.	What have I accepted or failed to accept within myself?

Exhaustion	Squandered energy.	What have I used up? What part of me is weary?
Ex-husband	Male aspect of self, either integrated or rejected.	What have I accepted or refused to accept within myself?
Explosion	Sudden, violent change.	What is ready to burst forth?
Extinct	No longer existing.	What part of me has been annihilated?
Extramarital sex *See also* Sex.	Illicit union.	What is lacking in my relationship with myself?
Ex-wife	Feminine aspect of self, either integrated or rejected.	What have I accepted or refused to accept within myself?

Image:	Associations:	Ask Yourself:
Eye *See also* Body parts.	Vision. Consciousness. Clarity.	What am I aware of? How do I see the world?
Face *See also* Body parts.	Identity. Ego. Self-image.	How do I appear?
Face-lift	Repair of self-image. Renewal. Vanity.	What part of my identity is ready for a make-over?
Fall (season)	Cycle of transformation. Results.	In what areas of my life am I ready to benefit from my past efforts?
Falling	Fear of failure. Loss of power. Loss of control.	Where in my life do I feel out of control? Where do I want to land?

False teeth
See Body parts: *teeth.*

Family	Kin. Group.	What am I ready to relate to? What do I feel part of?
Farting	Defensiveness. Passive aggression. Failure to digest experience.	Where in my life am I ready to be more direct?
Fat	Protection. Sensitivity. Safety.	What fears am I ready to lose?
Father	Authority. Control. Guidance. Recognition.	What do I take care of?
Fax	Contraction of space-time.	What am I ready to communicate instantly?
Fence	Boundary. Separation. Where differences meet.	What am I fencing in or fencing out?

Image:	Associations:	Ask Yourself:
Fetus	Potential. Conceived but not yet brought to birth.	What do I wish to produce?
Field	Expanse. Area of activity.	What am I ready to cultivate in myself?
Fight	Violent resolution. Release of energy.	What conflict am I building or releasing?
Films	The script or story being acted out. A means of distancing from events.	What is my story? What do I want to observe?
Finding	Discovery. Realization.	What am I ready to possess?
Finger *See also* Body parts.	Sensitivity. Awareness.	What am I touching?
Fire	Spirit. Energy. Unpolluted and cleansing.	In what areas of my life do I seek to be inspired, renewed?

Fireman	Protective masculine aspect of self.	What part of me needs to be rescued? What do I want to rescue?
Fireplace *See also* House.	Source of energy, heat, spiritual center of self.	What is central to me? What warms me?
Fish	Emotion. Freedom of movement in element of feeling. Inner self.	What do I feel?
Fishing *See also* Fish.	Seeking underneath or inside for nourishment.	What do I hope to catch?
Five *See also* Numbers.	Quintessence. Change. Celebration.	What is evolving in me?
Flag	Patriotism. Identification.	What am I loyal to?
Flasher	Frustrated sexuality. Exhibitionism.	In what ways am I denying my sexual needs or urges?

Image:	Associations:	Ask Yourself:
Flood *See also* Water.	Overflow of emotion.	What feelings are too much for me?
Floor *See also* House.	Foundation. Basic elements.	Where in my life do I want to create stability?
Flower	Beauty. Sexuality. Blossoming.	In what ways are my beauty and sexuality blossoming?
Flying	Most common ecstatic dream. A joyous combination of control and freedom.	Where in my life do I feel this joyous power?
Fog	Limited vision. Confusion.	Where in my life do I seek clarity?
Following	Pursuit.	What wants to be close to me? What am I ready to be close to?

Food
Nourishment. Security. Pleasure or greed.
What do I nourish in myself? What am I hungry for?

Foot
See also Body parts.
Grounding. Direction. Basic beliefs.
Where am I going?

Football
See Ball game; Sports.

Foreign
See also Countries.
Distant. Strange. Exotic.
What is boring about my life?

Foreigner
Expansion of self into unfamiliar realms.
What am I ready to explore in myself?

Forest
The realm of the unconscious. Natural forces.
What part of my inner nature am I ready to explore?

Image:	Associations:	Ask Yourself:
Fort	Defended self.	What defenses am I ready to examine?
Fountain *See also* Water.	Emotion springing forth. Freedom of emotional expression. Release.	What feelings are welling up in me?
Four *See also* Numbers; Square.	Stability. Matter. Strength. Worldly effort.	Where in my life am I most stable?
Freak	Abnormal. Unconventional.	What unique qualities am I ready to express?
Freeway	Travel. Route to freedom. Movement.	Where in my life am I free to move?
Friend	Aspect of self ready for integration.	What part of me is being integrated?

Frog
See also
Animals, wild.

Transformation.

What beauty lies within me?

Frozen
See also Water.

Preservation. Restraint.

What rigid feelings am I ready to dissolve?

Fruit

Product. Offspring.

What am I ready to harvest?

Funeral

The end or death of something.

What part of me is ready to go?

Furniture
See also House.

Identity. Attitudes. Beliefs.

How do I furnish the house of my self?

Gambling

Reward. Hope of recognition.

Where in my life am I ready to win?

Gangster

Criminal. Rule of force.

What new rules do I want to establish for myself?

Image:	Associations:	Ask Yourself:
Garbage	Cleaning and clearing up.	What am I ready to get rid of?
Garden	Inner self. Growth or blossoming.	What do I nurture in myself?
Gardener	Natural process. Growth.	What is growing in me?
Gay *See* Homosexual.		
Ghost	Spiritual aspect of self—sometimes feared. Memory.	What keeps coming back for me?
Gift	Recognition. Acknowledgment.	What part of myself do I wish to honor? What do I appreciate?
Giraffe *See also* Animals, wild.	Overview. Shy grace.	Where in my life am I ready to extend my vision?

Girl	Receptive or yin quality developing.	Where in my life am I learning to be receptive?
Girlfriend	Feminine ideal.	What do I admire in a female? What feminine aspect am I ready to integrate?
Glasses	Vision. Attitude. Belief.	What correction is necessary for me to see clearly?
Goat *See also* Animals, domestic.	Lusty vigor. Relentless energy. Omnivorous.	What am I determined to do?
God	Divine masculine. Sacred. Creator.	What do I hold sacred?
Goddess	Divine feminine. Compassion. Love.	What qualities do I worship?

Image:	Associations:	Ask Yourself:
Goose *See also* Animals, domestic.	Silly, aggressive, watchful.	Am I silly? Where in my life is my aggression apt to break out?
Gorilla *See also* Animals, wild.	Strength. Innocence. Rarity.	In what areas of my life am I ready to be strong and gentle?
Government	Administrative regulation. Control. Provider.	Where in my life do I feel controlled or taken care of?
Grandparent	Gentle authority. Kindness.	Where in my life do I seek support?
Grass	Natural protection. Ubiquity.	What part of myself can I always rely on?
Graveyard *See* Cemetery; Garden.		

Gray *See also* Colors.	Transition from one state to another. If clear, peace. If dull, fear.	What am I moving toward?
Green *See also* Colors.	Growth. Serenity. Healing through growth.	Where in my life am I growing?
Groom	Masculine activity and energy.	What union am I ready to commit myself to?
Guilty *or* guilty	Judgment.	What am I ready to forgive in myself or in others?
Gun	Violence. Aggression. Threat.	What threatens me? Where in my life do I want protection?
Hair *See also* Body parts.	Protection. Attraction. Sensuality.	What am I covering? What do I display?

Image:	Associations:	Ask Yourself:
Hairdresser	Work on self-image and self-esteem.	What am I ready to feel better about?
Hand *See also* Body parts.	Capacity. Competence. Help.	What am I ready to handle?
Handbag *See* Clothing: *purse.*		
Handicapped *See also* Cripple.	Restriction. Disadvantage.	What part of me is ready to be made whole?
Hanging	Holding back communication.	What am I ready to say or hear?
Harbor *See also* Water.	Shelter. Safety.	Where in my life do I find emotional peace?

Hat *See also* Clothing.	Opinons. Thoughts.	What thoughts or attitudes do I reveal?
Haunted house *See also* House.	Childhood fears. Prohibition. Past limitation.	What part of my past am I ready to purify or exorcise?
Head *See also* Body parts.	Intellect. Understanding. Superior.	What am I ready to understand?
Healer *or* healing	Restoration. Recovery.	Where in my life am I ready to be whole?
Heart *See also* Body parts.	Love. Security.	Where in my life am I ready to give and receive love?
Heat	Intense emotion. Stress.	Where do I need to cool off?

Image:	Associations:	Ask Yourself:
Heaven	Bliss. Transcendence.	Where in my life do I feel blessed?
Helicopter *See also* Vehicles.	Movement in many directions.	Where in my life do I want more freedom of movement?
Hell	Torment. Spiritual agony.	What am I ready to forgive in myself or others?
Helmet *See also* Clothing.	Protected opinions and attitudes.	What thoughts or opinions am I ready to change?
Herd *See* Crowd.		
Herpes	Misuse of sexual energy. Unwise sexual expression.	What worries me about sex?

High heels *See also* Clothing.	Glamour. Restriction. Sexual invitation.	How comfortable am I with conventional femininity?
High places	Attainment. Greater understanding.	What do I want to achieve? Where must I go to achieve it?
Highrise *See* Skyscraper.		
High school *See* High places; School.		
Highway *See* High places; Road.		
Hill	Easy achievement. Comfortable progress.	What is easy for me to do?
Hippy	Freedom. Excess. Rejection of conventional values.	What part of me desires or fears to be different?

Image:	Associations:	Ask Yourself:
Hitchhiker	Freedom. Irresponsibility.	What part of me wants a free ride?
Home *See also* House.	Center of being. Spiritual self.	Where does my spirit reside?
Homeless *See also* House.	Spiritual deprivation. Absence of security and stability.	What new structure am I seeking?
Homosexual *See also* Sex.	Union—or fear of union—with aspects of self.	What part of my femininity or masculinity do I seek to merge with?
Hook *See also* Fishing.	To ensnare. Trap.	What do I want to catch?
Hooker *See* Prostitute.		

Horse *See also* Animals, domestic; Vehicles.	Swift. Usually elegant. Feeling of developed consciousness. Sometimes unexpressed sexuality.	How do I feel about my power? What natural force am I suppressing or expressing?
Horse, flying *or* **winged** *See also* Animals, domestic.	Soaring consciousness. Limitless nature of self.	What part of me is ready to soar?
Hospital	Healing. Confinement.	What am I ready to heal?
Hostage	Imprisonment as security.	What do I get from holding myself or others back?
Hot *See* Heat.		
Hotel	Transitional aspect of identity.	What part of me is in transit?

Image:	Associations:	Ask Yourself:
House *See also subheadings.*	Being. The house of self.	What do I believe or fear about myself?
—*apartment*	A part of the total house of self.	What part of myself do I occupy?
—*attic*	Higher consciousness. Memory. Stored-up past.	What is "up there" that I want or fear to explore?
—*basement*	Below. The unconscious.	What part of my unconscious is ready to be seen?
—*bathroom*	Place of cleansing and release.	What am I ready to release?
—*bedroom*	Privacy. Rest. Intimacy.	What is my inner reality?
—*castle*	Fortified but noble self.	What walls am I ready to remove?

—ceiling	Upper limits.	Where in my life am I ready to raise my limits?
—cottage	Cozy, familiar house of the self.	What part of me wants to be snug?
—dining room	The ritual of eating. Formality.	What sustenance do I require?
—door	Access. Movement from one area to another.	What space am I ready to enter or to keep private?
—fireplace	Source of energy, heat, spiritual center of self.	What is central to me? What warms me?
—floor	Foundation. Basic elements.	Where in my life do I want to create stability?
—furniture	Identity. Attitudes. Beliefs.	How do I furnish the house of my self?

Image:	Associations:	Ask Yourself:
—*haunted house*	Childhood fears. Prohibition. Past limitation.	What part of my past am I ready to purify or exorcise?
—*home*	Center of being. Spiritual self.	Where does my spirit reside?
—*homeless*	Spiritual deprivation. Absence of security and stability.	What new structure am I seeking?
—*hut*	Basic or primitive needs. Retreat. Humility.	Where in my life am I ready to be humble?
—*kitchen*	Nourishment. Productivity.	What's cooking?
—*living room*	Central space of the house of self.	What is central to my being?
—*mansion*	Expansive residence of the self.	What part of me needs more room?

—*palace* Potential kingdom of the self. How can I fulfill my potential?

—*porch* Intersection of self with world. Where in my life am I ready to be more approachable?

—*rafters* Protective support. What supports my higher consciousness?

—*roof* Above. Protection. Covering. Where in my life am I ready to expand my limitations?

—*stairs* Ascent. Going higher. Aspiration. Descent. Grounding. What do I want to rise or descend to?

—*window* Vision. Seeing and being seen. What am I willing to see? What do I wish to reveal or conceal?

Hugging Loving protection. Acknowledgment. What part of me needs more attention?
See also Sex.

Image:	Associations:	Ask Yourself:
Hurricane	Destructive emotions.	What powerful feelings am I ready to experience?
Husband	Yang aspect of self. Partner.	What am I committed to?
Hut *See also* House.	Basic or primitive needs. Retreat. Humility.	Where in my life am I ready to be humble?
Hydrofoil *See also* Travel; Vehicles.	Soaring above the sea of feeling.	What emotions no longer inhibit me?
Hypodermic *See also* Injection.		
Ice *See also* Water.	A rigid feeling state. Frozen.	What feelings are locked within or ready to be melted away?

Ice pick	Cold feelings.	What feelings are frozen in me?
Incest *See also* Sex.	Fear of love.	Am I ready to be sexually mature?
Injection	Forceful introduction. Need.	What must I have?
Insect *See* Bug.		
Intercourse *See also* Sex.	Union. Release. Pleasure. Creation.	What do I want or fear to merge with?
Invalid *See also* Cripple; Handicapped.	Infirmity. Work on long-standing weakness or illness.	What old limitations am I ready to heal?
Invasion	Forced entry. Attack.	What part of me is ready to be more assertive?
Island	Solitude. Separation. Escape. May be enjoyable or lonely.	What do I separate myself from?

Image:	Associations:	Ask Yourself:
Jail *See* Prison.		
Jaw *See also* Body parts.	Will. Relentless anger.	Where in my life must I dominate? Where am I ready to yield?
Jellyfish	Spineless. Passive aggression.	Where in my life am I ready to express myself more forcefully?
Jesus *See also* Christ.	Human aspect of divinity. Salvation. Healing.	What part of me is ready to be saved?
Jewel	Treasure. Essence. Precious.	What is valuable? What do I value in myself?
Journey *See also* Travel.	Liberation. Movement toward inner center.	What is my inner process?

Judge

Decision making. Wisdom or condemnation.

What decision am I ready to make? What part of me is wise and knowledgeable?

Junkyard

Discarded ideas, attitudes, beliefs.

What value can I find in the past?

Key

Solution. Access.

What problem am I ready to solve?

Killing
See Murder.

King

Noble aspect of masculinity.

Where in my life am I ready to express masculine power?

Kissing
See also Sex.

Intimacy. Affection. Greeting.

What or whom do I wish to be close to?

Image:	Associations:	Ask Yourself:
Kitchen *See also* House.	Nourishment. Productivity.	What's cooking?
Knee *See also* Body parts.	Flexibility. Humility.	Where in my life do I need to bend?
Knife	Aggression. Severing. Anger.	What do I want to cut out?
Knots	Restriction. Holding together.	What is tied up in me?
Laboratory	Exploration. Detached examination.	What am I searching for?
Labyrinth *See* Maze.		
Ladder	Reaching upward.	How high am I ready to climb?

Lake *See also* Water.	Contained emotion. Often a sense of tranquility or peace.	What feelings do I comfortably contain?
Laughing	Communication of joy.	What is my source of happiness and freedom?
Lawyer *See* Attorney.		
Leg *See also* Body parts.	Support. Movement.	What supports me? Am I getting somewhere?
Library	Knowledge. Records. Research. The past.	What does the past have to tell me?
Light	Illumination. Vision.	What am I ready to see?
Lightning	Flash of illumination. Sudden vision.	What is awakening in me?

Image:	Associations:	Ask Yourself:
Limousine *See also* Vehicles.	Luxurious power. Extravagance.	Where in my life am I ready to be conspicuous in my expression of power?
Lion *See also* Animals, wild.	Nobility. Strength. Pride.	Where does courage dwell in me?
Little	Smaller than usual. Reduced. Insignificant.	Where in my life do I feel diminished? What am I ready to reduce?
Living room *See also* House.	Central space of the house of self.	What is central to my being?
Lizard *See also* Animals, wild.	Cold-blooded. Reptilian.	Where in my life am I ready to show more warmth?

Term	Definition	Questions
Locker *See also* School.	Storage. Safekeeping.	What have I stored away? What am I ready to remember?
Lost	Without direction. Missing.	Where in my life am I lacking in confidence?
Lottery *See* Gambling.		
Lover	The idealized inner self. Anima. Animus.	What part of my larger self is ready to be integrated?
Luggage *See also* Baggage.	Belongings. Beliefs.	What am I taking with me? What am I ready to leave behind?
Lungs *See also* Body parts.	Breath of life. Freedom.	In what ways is my life ready to expand?

Image:	Associations:	Ask Yourself:
Machine	Automation. Convenience. Repetition.	What burdensome work am I ready to be free of?
Maggot *See* Worm.		
Magician	Work on command of inner and outer worlds or forces. Transformation.	What powers do I control or fear?
Mail	News. Guidance.	What do I want to hear or learn?
Mailman	Work on communication.	What do I want to hear or say?
Makeup	Image. Feminine projection.	Who do I show to the world?
Mall	Central resources. Community. Consumption.	What needs or desires do I share with others?

Term	Meaning	Question
Man	Yang aspect. Active.	Where in my life am I ready to be more assertive?
Mandala	The totality of the self. Wholeness.	Where in my life am I ready to express my totality of being?
Mansion *See also* House.	Expansive residence of the self.	What part of me needs more room?
Map	Guidance. Directions.	What information do I need to make my journey?
Marriage	Union. Commitment.	What am I ready to join or commit myself to?
Mask	Disguise. Persona. Attitudes.	What do I hide? What do I display?

Image:	Associations:	Ask Yourself:
Masturbation *See also* Sex.	Self-love.	What part of myself am I ready to accept and love?
Maze	Puzzle. Labyrinth.	What intricate problems am I ready to solve?
Meat	Essential nourishment. Sometimes a need to survive.	What must I do to survive? Where am I ready to trust?
Mechanic	Repair. Make good. Work on what has been damaged.	What damage am I ready to restore?
Medicine	Healing. Antidote.	Where in my life am I ready to be healthy and whole?
Menstruation	Power or fear of feminine identity.	Where am I ready to express more natural power?

Mermaid *or* merman	Emotional part of identity.	What do I want to feel?
Microwave	Accelerated processing.	What am I in a hurry for?
Milk *See also* Food.	Maternal love. Sustenance. Kindness.	What part of me is developing and seeks nourishment?
Minister	Work on compassion or care giving.	Where in my life am I ready to be more understanding?
Mirror	Image. Identity.	What part of me is reflected? What am I ready to see?
Mist *See also* Water.	Delicate expanse of feeling. Cool and comfortable.	What emotional field surrounds me?

Image:	Associations:	Ask Yourself:
Mob *See also* Crowd.	Loss of organizing principle or control.	Where in my life am I ready to command my conflicting desires?
Mobile phone *See* Car; Cellular phone; Telephone.		
Monastery	Spiritual community. Withdrawal from worldly affairs.	Where in my life do I seek to join with my spiritual peers?
Money	Security. Riches.	What do I value?
Monk	Retreat. Spiritual life.	What part of me needs to withdraw from life's demands?
Monkey *See also* Animals, wild.	Dexterity. Mischief. Humor.	What part of me is almost human?

Monster Denied self. Threat. What do I fear in myself?

Moon Emotion. Reflection. Inner self. What feelings do I reflect?

Motel
See Hotel.

Mother Nurturance. Approval or disapproval. What do I care for in myself?

Motorcycle
See also
Vehicles. Virility. Vigor. Display. How hot am I? Where in my life am I ready to be more masterful?

Mountain Aspiration. Success through effort. What am I ready to achieve?

Mouse
See also
Animals, wild. Meek nature. Quiet. Minor problems. Inner feelings. Shyness. What small troubles are gnawing away at me?

Image:	Associations:	Ask Yourself:
Mouth *See also* Body parts.	Nourishment. New attitudes.	What am I ready to take in? What am I ready to express?
Movies *See Films.*		
Movie star	Glamour. Recognition. Fame.	What part of me is ready to be in the spotlight?
Mud	Stuck feelings. If good, fertility; if bad, dirty emotions.	What am I ready to wash away? What is growing?
Mule *See also* Animals, domestic.	Obstinate. Intractable. Stamina.	Where in my life am I ready to persevere?
Murder	Violent completion.	What will I do anything to end?

Muscles *See also* Body parts.	Power. Strength.	In what aspects of my life am I ready to be more powerful?
Music	Harmony. Expression.	What am I integrating?
Naked	Exposed. Vulnerable.	Where am I ready to be seen?
Native	Intuitive self. Harmony with nature. Primitive being.	Where in my life do I seek alignment with nature?
Nausea *See* Seasick; Vomit.		
Navy	Command of feeling. Sometimes homosexual undertones.	What emotions am I ready to command?
Nazi	Totalitarian control. Sentimentality.	What extreme reactions am I ready to adjust?

Image:	Associations:	Ask Yourself:
Neck *See also* Body parts.	Flexibility, especially of vision.	What can I see if I make a small adjustment?
Negro *See* African-American.		
Nerd	Insignificant but smart. Absence of charm.	Where in my life am I ready to be as attractive as I am smart?
Nets	Safety. Entrapment.	Where in my life am I ready to be fearless?
Night	Mystery. Unconscious contents. Inner vision.	What darkness am I ready to penetrate?
Nightclub *See also* Night.	Stimulation. Entertainment.	What excitement do I seek?

Nightgown
See Clothing: *dress*; Night.

Nine
See also
Numbers.

Hidden blessings. Completion. Compassion.

What is revealed to me?

North

Death and transformation. Effort.

What do I want to end whatever the cost?

Nose
See also
Body parts.

Instinctive knowledge.

How does it smell to me? What do I know without knowing?

Nuclear bomb
See Atom bomb.

Nude
See Naked.

Numbers
See subheadings.

We lack a consistent cultural tradition for the interpretation of numbers. If a number appears repeatedly in a dream, or if it is

Image:	Associations:	Ask Yourself:
	highlighted, first ask yourself what personal significance it has for you. It may refer to an important date in your life, to a well-remembered address or birth date, or to other events or experiences. Begin by identifying these personal associations. Below is a common interpretation of numbers one through ten, with the addition of numbers eleven, twenty-two, and thirty-three. Dream consciousness is always hungry for new material; this system can easily be digested if you find it nourishing.	
—one	Beginning. Oneness. Essence. Individual will.	Who am I?
—two	Duality. Opposition. Balance. Partnership.	How do I relate?
—three	Trinity. Balance of opposites. Sociability.	How do I integrate my differences?
—four	Stability. Matter. Potential for Sudden change. Worldly effort.	Where in my life am I most stable?

—*five*	Quintessence. Change. Celebration.	What is evolving in me?
—*six*	Expansion. Organization. Harmony. Domesticity.	What am I ready to commit to?
—*seven*	Energy given form. Cycles of growth. Discipline.	What am I ready to learn?
—*eight*	Eternity. Abundance. Power. Cosmic consciousness.	What am I willing to receive?
—*nine*	Hidden blessings. Completion. Compassion.	What is revealed to me?
—*ten*	New beginning on a higher octave.	What have I learned?
—*eleven*	Inspiration. Revolution. Higher octave of two.	What am I ready to change?
—*twenty-two*	Earthly mission. Self and others.	What do I trust?
—*thirty-three*	Salvation and temptation.	Where in my life have I succeeded or failed?

Image:	Associations:	Ask Yourself:
Nun	Retreat. Spiritual life.	What part of me needs to withdraw from life's demands?
Nurse	Healing care. Compassion.	What part of me needs to be cared for, or needs to care for others?
Oasis	Place of refuge and relaxation.	Where in my life do I seek a sanctuary?
Ocean *See also* Water.	Vast, limitless feeling. Sometimes an overwhelming emotion. Rich with abundant life.	What part of me relates to such vastness?
Octopus	Shy. Grasping.	What do I need to hold on to?

Odor
See Smell.

Office — Workplace. Professional aspect of self. — What am I working on or with?

Old — Maturity. Degeneration. — What is complete for me? What am I ready to replace?

One
See also Numbers. — Beginning. Oneness. Essence. Individual will. — Who am I?

Open — Opportunity. Potential. — What choice am I ready to make?

Operation
See Surgery.

Oral sex
See also Sex. — Gratification. Pleasure. — What part of me wants to give or receive gratification?

Image:	Associations:	Ask Yourself:
Orange *See also* Colors.	Emotion. Stimulation. Healing.	What am I feeling?
Orgy *See also* Sex.	Indiscriminate union.	Where in my life am I ready to experience the oneness of all?
Oriental *See also* East.	Eastern wisdom. Subtlety.	Where in my life is wisdom developing for me?
Outlaw	Rebellion. Adventure.	What freedom do I seek?
Owl	Wisdom. Vision.	What part of me is naturally wise?
Oyster *See also* Food.	Tender inside, hard outside. Sexual stimulation.	What am I hungry for?
Pack	Load. Burden. Equipment.	What do I carry with me?

Packing	Preparation for movement. Sorting or storing old ideas.	What do I want to take or leave behind?
Pager	Accessibility. Availability.	What part of me is always on call?
Pain	Conflict. Problem. Suffering.	What hurts me? What parts of my self are denied?
Painting See also Art; Artist.	Transforming. Decorating.	What do I wish to change or improve?
Palace See also House.	Potential kingdom of the self.	How can I fulfill my potential?
Pan See also Satyr.	Divinity of nature. Unleashing.	What elemental aspects of my nature am I coming to terms with?

Image:	Associations:	Ask Yourself:
Panties *See also* Clothing.	Private self. Sexual identity.	What are my hidden feelings? What am I ready to expose?
Pants *See* Trousers.		
Parade	Fanciful display. Options.	What part of me wants to be seen?
Paradise *See* Heaven.		
Paralysis	Resistance. No change or growth.	What move am I preparing to make?
Parasite	Work on independence.	Where am I ready to fend for myself?
Paratrooper	Invasion. The thrill of physical danger.	What territory do I want to encounter?

Parrot	Imitative. Humorous. Exotic.	Where in my life do I lack originality?
Party	Celebration. Festivity.	What am I ready to celebrate?
Passport	Freedom of movement. Identity.	What part of me wants to expand and explore?
Pastry *See also* **Cake.**	Luxury. Indulgence. Sweetness.	What do I crave? Is there enough sweetness in my life?
Path	Life's direction.	What do I feel about my chosen route?
Pattern	Established order.	What beliefs am I examining?
Peacock	Pride and vanity. Display.	What do I wish to have seen or admired?

Image:	Associations:	Ask Yourself:
Peak *See also* Mountain.	Point of success. Achievement.	What am I heading for?
Pearl *See also* Jewel.	Purity. Treasure. Transforming irritation to beauty.	What do I value? How is it created?
Pedestal	Admiration. Worship.	What do I look up to?
Pee *or* peeing *See* Urinating.		
Penis *See also* Body parts.	Male sexuality. Yang power.	How is my power expressed?
Performing	Accomplishment. Achievement.	Where in my life do I seek recognition?
Period *See* Menstruation.		

Photograph — Image. Vision. Memory. — What do I remember? How do I see the world?

Photographer
See also Camera. — Work on world image. — What image of the world do I want to preserve?

Pig
See also Animals, domestic. — Greedy. Smart. Sometimes slovenly, sometimes fastidious. — Am I grabbing more than I need or can use? Do I clean up my own mess?

Pillow — Comfort. Intimacy. — What part of me seeks encouragement?

Pimples — Ugliness. Small bursts of anger. — How am I ready to be less sensitive?

Pink
See also Colors. — Affection. Love. — To what am I responding?

Pirate — Outlaw. Rejection of social rules and obligations. — What rules do I reject? Where do I feel restricted by society?

Image:	Associations:	Ask Yourself:
Plague	Universal disorder or disease.	What system do I believe is breaking down?
Plane *See also* Vehicles.	Rapid movement across great distance.	Am I in a hurry for change?
Planets	Cosmic harmony and influence. Celestial order.	Am I in or out of harmony with heavenly power?
Plants	Nature. Natural process. Fertility.	What is growing in me?
Plastic	Artificiality. Cheap substitute. Resilience.	What is the real thing?
Play	Performance. Script or production of life.	What changes in my life script am I considering?
Plumber *or* plumbing	Work on emotional release.	What part of me needs clearing out or replacing?

Poison	Destructive actions or thoughts.	What no longer nourishes me?
Police	Work on order or control.	Where in my life do I seek order or fear control?
Politician	Work on policy. Choosing sides. Manipulation.	What side am I on? Where do I want to win?
Poor	Limited expression of resources.	What am I ready to develop?
Porch *See also* House.	Intersection of self with world.	Where in my life am I ready to be more approachable?
Porpoise *See* Dolphin.		
Praying	Communion. Seeking help.	Where in my life am I ready to surrender?

Image:	Associations:	Ask Yourself:
Pregnancy	New life. Fecundity.	What am I preparing to produce?
Present *See* Gift.		
President	Leadership or lack of leadership.	Where in my life am I ready or reluctant to lead?
Priest	Work on spiritual or religious well-being. Release.	What am I ready to forgive?
Prince	Noble aspect of self. Refined masculinity.	What do I admire or seek in men, or in myself?
Princess	Noble aspect of self. Refined feminity.	What do I admire to seek in women, or in myself?

Prison	Punishment. Confinement.	Where have I done wrong?
Procession *See also* Parade.	Ceremonial march. Pomp.	What beliefs am I ready to formalize or observe?
Prostitute	If negative, misuse of sexuality. If positive, sexual healing.	What do I need to feel sexually healthy?
Pruning	Elimination of old growth.	What old stuff am I ready to cut away?
Psychokinesis	Power of consciousness over matter.	In what ways am I ready to take control of the world?
Pub *See* Tavern.		
Punks	Alienation. Protest.	What part of me wants more love and attention?

Image:	Associations:	Ask Yourself:
Purple *See* Violet.		
Purse *See also* Clothing.	Feminine self. Sometimes sexual identity. Security.	What am I holding onto? What part of myself do I value?
Queen	Noble aspect of femininity.	Where in my life am I ready to express feminine power?
Quest *See also* Searching.	Adventure. Soul seeking.	What part of me holds the answer?
Quicksand	Insecurity. Instability.	Where in my life do I want a stronger foundation?

Rabbit *See also* Animals, wild; Animals, domestic.	Fertility. Luck. Insecurity.	Where in my life am I ready to be productive?
Radio	Story about reality. Communication.	What am I ready to hear or say?
Rafters *See also* House.	Protective support.	What supports my higher consciousness?
Railroad *See* Train.		
Rain *See also* Water.	Release of emotion. May be gentle and nourishing or dramatically threatening.	What feelings are pouring down on me?
Rape *See also* Sex.	Forced union.	What do I fear being forced to unite with?

Image:	Associations:	Ask Yourself:
Rapist *See also* Sex.	Forcing union.	Where in my life do I feel my love is rejected?
Rat *See also* Animals, wild.	Street smarts. Clever. Sneaky and untrustworthy.	Where in my life do I fear betrayal? Can I trust myself?
Raven	Magic. Omen. Sagacity.	What is the message?
Red *See also* Colors.	Energy. Vigor. Passion.	What is my source of energy or strength?
Refrigerator	Chilling to preserve.	What do I want to save?
Repairing	Work on what has been damaged.	What am I ready to fix?
Restaurant	Place of nourishment. Choices.	What do I want to order?

Retarded	Work on development and training or education.	Where in my life do I want to catch up with others? Where do I fear being behind?
Rhinestone	Imitation. Cheap substitute.	Where in my life am I ready for the real thing?
Ring	Pledge. Commitment. Promise.	What union do I seek?
River *See also* Water.	Flowing and active. May include dangerous rapids; may be smooth and tranquil.	What feelings are actively moving within me?
Road	Direction. Life's path.	Where am I going?
Robbery *See* Theft.		
Robot	Mechanical aspect of self.	What freedom do I seek?

Image:	Associations:	Ask Yourself:
Rocket *See also* Spaceship.	Breaking free of physical limits. Exploration of inner space.	What limitations am I ready to transcend?
Rodeo	Exhibition of skill. Human control of animal force.	Where am I ready to display my skill at mastering wild forces?
Roller coaster	Ups and downs. Thrills. Wild but safe ride.	What excitement do I crave?
Roof *See also* House.	Above. Protection. Covering.	Where in my life am I ready to expand my limitations?
Rooster	Aggressive masculinity. Conceit.	What do I want to crow about?
Rug *See* Carpet.		

Running	Rapid movement. Escape. Joy of the physical.	What moves me?
R.V. *See also* Vehicles.	The joy of power. Rugged amusement.	Where in my life am I ready to enjoy the expression of power?
Sage	Work on wisdom or understanding.	Where in my life do I want to apply thought and good judgment?
Sailor *See also* Navy.	Navigating emotional seas.	What feelings am I taking charge of?
Salesperson *See also* Shopping.	Service. Availability.	What do I want to include in my life?
Santa Claus	Belief. Getting what you want.	What do I believe I want?

Image:	Associations:	Ask Yourself:
Satellite	Message. Expansion through technology.	What distant news am I ready to hear?
Satyr *See also* Goat; Man.	Work on union of intellect with animal passion.	Where in my life am I integrating my mind and my body? Where do I seek sexual freedom?
Scalp *See* Body parts: *skin, hair.*		
Scar	Healed wound. Incomplete release of emotional hurt.	What am I ready to heal completely?
School	Education. Discipline.	What do I need to learn? What have I already learned and no longer need to study?
Scientist	Work on understanding or knowledge.	What do I want to comprehend or describe?

Scissors	Feminine weapon. Separation.	What do I wish to cut out?
Scorpion	Destructive feelings, thoughts, words.	Where in my life am I ready to express my authority and power?
Sea *See* Ocean; Water.		
Searching *See also* Quest.	Recognition of desire or wants. Acknowledgment of need.	What am I finally ready to find?
Seashell *See* Shell.		
Seasick	Sickening emotions.	What feelings am I ready to get rid of?
Seaweed	Growth within emotion. Can be nourishing or strangling.	What is developing in my sea of feeling?

Image:	Associations:	Ask Yourself:
Seat belt *See also* Vehicles.	Safety Restraint.	What holds my power in check?
Secretary	Organization. Order. Help.	Where in my life do I need to get organized?
Seed	Beginning. Source of greater being.	What or where do I wish to develop?
Seeking *See* Searching.		
Seizures	Extreme agitation. Spasmodic movement.	Where in my life do I fear or seek control?
Senile	Work on declining abilities.	What is no longer important to me?

Serpent
See Snake.

Seven
See also
Numbers.

Energy given form. Cycles of growth. Discipline.

What am I ready to learn?

Sewer

Accumulation of negativity. Release.

What junk am I ready to get rid of?

Sewing

Joining together. Repair.

What do I want to create or restore?

Sex
See subheadings.

—*anal*

Submission. Union without issue.

To what or to whom do I want or fear to yield?

—*arousal*

Stimulation. Availability.

What do I want to respond to?

Image:	Associations:	Ask Yourself:
—*bestiality*	Union with animal passions or instincts.	What basic aspects of myself do I fear or deny?
—*erection*	Creative power. Fertility.	What do I want to do or to make?
—*extramarital*	Illicit union.	What is lacking in my relationship with myself?
—*homosexual*	Union—or fear of union—with aspects of self.	What part of my femininity or masculinity do I seek to merge with?
—*hugging*	Loving protection. Acknowledgment.	What part of me needs more attention?
—*incest*	Fear of love.	Am I ready to be sexually mature?
—*intercourse*	Union. Release. Pleasure. Creation.	What do I want or fear to merge with?

—*kissing*	Intimacy. Affection. Greeting.	What or whom do I wish to be close to?
—*masturbation*	Self-love.	What part of myself am I ready to love and accept?
—*oral*	Gratification. Pleasure.	What part of me wants to give or receive gratification?
—*orgy*	Indiscriminate union.	Where in my life am I ready to experience the oneness of all?
—*rape*	Forced union.	What do I fear being forced to unite with?
—*rapist*	Forcing union.	Where in my life do I feel my love is rejected?
Shadow	Hidden. Dark side of image.	What am I ready to illuminate?

Image:	Associations:	Ask Yourself:
Shampoo *See* Soap; Hair.		
Shark	Dangers lurking in emotion.	What powerful feeling is threatening me?
Sheep *See also* Animals, domestic.	Conformity.	What am I following?
Shell	Protection. Can be limiting or covering. Beauty of form.	Which feelings do I need to protect? What structures do I value?
Shield	Protection. Security. Defense.	Where in my life am I ready to be more vulnerable?
Shipwreck *See* Boat; Wreck.		

Shirt
See also
Clothing.

Upper, as opposed to lower, self. Emotions.

What feelings do I consider appropriate?

Shit
See Excrement.

Shoes
See also
Clothing.

General situation. Grounding.

How well do I connect with the world?

Shooting

Destroying aspects of self.

What do I want to get rid of?

Shopping

Finding what you want. Options.

What am I ready to take home?

Shorts
See also
Clothing.

Private self. Sexual identity.

What are my hidden feelings? What am I ready to expose?

Image:	Associations:	Ask Yourself:
Shoulders *See also* Body parts.	Strength or burdens.	What am I ready to carry? What is too heavy for me?
Shower	Cleansing. Release down the drain.	What do I want to wash away?
Shrimp	Insignificant. Of small value.	Where in my life am I ready to feel more worthy?
Shrinking	Inadequacy. Too small.	Where in my life—or by whom—do I feel diminished?
Silver	Precious. Flexible. Spiritual strength.	What part of my spirit needs strengthening?
Singing	Joyous celebration. Praise. Communication of feeling.	What do I want to celebrate or communicate?

Sister	Feminine self. Fellowship.	What do I admire or judge in myself?
Six *See also* **Numbers.**	Expansion. Organization. Harmony. Domesticity.	What am I ready to commit to?
Skateboard	Youthful expression of power. Joyous freedom of movement.	Where in my life do I seek rejuvenation?
Skating *See also* Ice.	Rapid movement with great ease. Grace.	What am I ready to move across with ease?
Skiing *See also* Snow.	High speed, active movement. Physical skill and balance.	What part of me is ready to enjoy greater freedom of movement?
Skin *See also* Body parts.	Surface of the self. Sensitivity. Connection between inner and outer.	What is on the surface?

Image:	Associations:	Ask Yourself:
Skirt *See also* Clothing.	Lower self. Passions.	What signals am I sending?
Skunk *See also* Animals, wild.	Passive aggression.	Where in my life do I feel the need to protect myself?
Sky	Limitless freedom. Expansion.	Where in my life can I be without limits?
Skyscraper	Lofty aspiration. Worldly goals.	What do I wish to achieve? How high am I ready to climb?
Sleeping	Unconscious. Deep relaxation and rest.	What part of me is ready to awaken?
Small *See* Little.		

Smell	Intuition based on senses.	What smells bad or good in this situation?
Smoking *or* smoke *See also* Cigarette.	Restricted vision. Residue. Screen.	What is hidden? What do I want to hide?
Snake *See also* Animals, wild.	Energy. The serpent power of kundalini. Sexuality.	What energy am I ready to express or understand?
Snow	Purity. Emotion in suspension. Clarity. Ends and beginnings.	What is over? Where in my life do I want a fresh start?
Soap	Cleansing. Purification.	Do I need to clean up my act?
Soldier	Work on confrontation.	What am I ready to challenge? Where in my life do I fear challenge?

Image:	Associations:	Ask Yourself:
Son	Youthful, masculine aspect of self.	Where in my life am I ready to express youthful power?
South	Ease. Freedom from constraint. Relaxation.	What part of me seeks release?
Spaceship *See also* Rocket.	Exploration of consciousness or inner realms. Transcendence of physical limitations.	What greater consciousness am I seeking or making contact with?
Speaking	Communication. Message.	What am I telling myself?
Spear *See also* Weapon.	Wounding projectile. Attack from a short distance.	What fears am I ready to look at more closely?
Sphere *See* Circle.		

Spider	The dark feminine force. Spinner of webs. Patience. Organization.	Do I fear or admire these qualities in myself?
Spine *See also* Body parts.	Support. Responsibility.	What holds me up?
Spiral	Dynamic movement. Evolution. Cycles.	Where in my life am I growing and expanding?
Sports	Playing the game. Honor.	What game am I playing?
Spring *See also* Water.	Source. Beginning.	Where in my life am I allowing my feelings new expression?
Spring (season)	Cycle of growth. Generation.	What am I incubating?
Spy	Work on secrecy.	Where in my life am I ready to open up?

Image:	Associations:	Ask Yourself:
Square *See also* Four.	Stability. Matter. Strength. Sudden change.	What in my life is stable for me? Where is my stability about to change?
Squirrel *See also* Animals, wild.	Hoarding. Running in place.	Where in my life am I ready to feel more secure?
Stabbing	Fear of betrayal.	Where in my life am I ready to be more trusting?
Stairs *See also* House.	Ascent. Going higher. Aspiration. Descent. Grounding.	What do I want to rise or descend to?
Star	Source of light or illumination. Spiritual awakening.	Where in my life am I ready to shine forth?
Statue	Representation. Image.	What content do I wish to give form to?

Steak
See Meat.

Stealing
See Theft.

Stink
See Smell.

Stomach
See also
Body parts.
Digestion of information or circumstances. Understanding. What value can I receive from my experience?

Store
Resources. Variety. Choice. What new things am I seeking?

Storm
Tumultuous change. What forces are struggling within me?

Strangling
Holding back communication. What am I ready to say or hear?

Image:	Associations:	Ask Yourself:
Stream *See also* Water.	The flow of feeling.	What feelings flow comfortably within me?
Street *See* Road.		
Stripes	Order. Organized effort.	What line am I willing or unwilling to follow?
Stump	Interrupted or blocked growth.	Have I been growing in the wrong direction? Do I feel thwarted?
Submarine	Means of exploring unconscious or emotional states.	What feelings am I ready to examine?
Subway	Rapid movement through the unconscious	What powerful drives can I make conscious use of?

Sugar	Sweetness. Indulgence. Sometimes forbidden pleasure.	What pleasures do I deny myself?
Suicide	Self-destruction. Giving up part of the self.	What part of me must go? What do I want to quit?
Suitcase	*See* Baggage; Luggage.	
Summer	Cycle of fruition. Fullness of growth.	What am I producing?
Sun	Energy. Light. Source. Life-giving power.	What do I wish or fear to receive?
Sunrise	Awakening. Beginning. Hope.	Where in my life am I ready to start over?
Sunset	Rest. Completion of the cycle. Release.	What have I accomplished?
Surfing	Riding the waves of feeling.	What powerful emotions am I ready to enjoy?
	See also Water.	

Image:	Associations:	Ask Yourself:
Surgery	Work on healing.	What part of me wants to be well?
Swamp *See also* Water.	Overwhelming, turgid feelings.	What old emotional patterns are beginning to change for me?
Swelling	Out-of-control expansion.	What pressure am I ready to release?
Swimming *See also* Water.	Movement through feeling, often with feelings of accomplishment. Emotion as environment.	What emotional state is deeply satisfying to me? What emotional support do I seek?
Swimming pool *See also* Water.	The water of feeling contained by cultural constructs. Safety.	What feeling do I wish to contain safely?
Swimming underwater	Submersion in emotion.	What feelings am I submerged in?

Sword *See also* Weapon.	Cutting away, especially the past or falsity.	What old ideas or beliefs am I prepared to sever?
Table	Place of activity.	What am I ready to examine or to do?
Talking	Communication.	What am I ready to express? To whom or what do I want to communicate?
Tan *See also* Colors.	Convention. Hard work. Propriety.	In what ways do I seek or avoid respectability?
Tank	Armor. Destructive protection. Mobile threat.	What is dangerous in my expression of power?
Tattoo	Unorthodox self-expression. Display.	What strange message am I ready to convey?

Image:	Associations:	Ask Yourself:
Tavern *See also* Bars.	Conviviality. Relaxation. Indulgence.	What fellowship do I thirst for?
Teacher	Learning. Discipline.	What do I want to know?
Tear gas	Torturous feelings. Smothered by suffering.	What deep pain am I ready to wash away?
Teenager *See* Adolescent.		
Teeth *See also* Body parts.	Independence. Power. Ability to nourish and communicate.	Where in my life do I fear dependence? What do I wish to say?
Telephone	Communication at a distance.	To whom or what do I want to reach out?
Telescope	Distant vision.	What do I want to observe more closely?

Television	Image or story about reality. Means of observing events.	What story am I creating? What do I want to observe?
Ten *See also* Numbers.	New beginning on a higher octave. Groups.	What have I learned?
Tent *See also* House.	Temporary house of the self.	What natural part of myself do I wish to reconnect with?
Terrorist	Violence born of frustration.	Where in my life do I feel my power is thwarted?
Test	Ordeal or examination.	What abilities or knowledge am I ready to demonstrate?
Testicles *See also* Body parts.	Yang power. Masculinity.	What power am I ready to express?

Image:	Associations:	Ask Yourself:
Theft	Lack. Need. Judgment.	What do I fear I can't have or don't deserve? What am I afraid of losing?
Therapist	Work on self-acceptance and love.	What parts of myself are ready for integration?
Thigh *See also* Body parts.	Power of movement.	Am I strong enough to get where I want to go?
Thirty-three *See also* Numbers.	Salvation and temptation.	Where in my life have I succeeded or failed?
Three *See also* Numbers; Triangle.	Trinity. Balance of opposites. Sociability.	How do I integrate my differences?

Throat *See also* Body parts.	Communication. Trust. Creativity.	What am I ready to hear and say?
Thugs	Ugly forms of power. Misuse of energy.	Where in my life am I ready to clean up my act? How is power threatening to me?
Ticket	Means of admission.	What new experience or destination am I heading for?
Tidal wave *See also* Water.	Overwhelming emotion.	What feelings are threatening to me?
Tiger *See also* Animals, wild.	Power. Wild beauty. Sexual force.	What is dangerous in me?
Tires *See also* Vehicles.	Cushion. Shock absorption.	Where in my life do I need to smooth my way?

Image:	Associations:	Ask Yourself:
Toad *See also* Animals, wild.	Infectious ugliness.	How or why have I concealed my true beauty?
Toe *See also* Body parts.	Beginning, especially of movement.	Where am I preparing to go?
Toilet *See* Bathroom; Excrement; Urinating.		
Tongue *See also* Body parts.	The pleasure of taste.	What am I eager to try?
Tools	Equipment. Abilities. Capacity.	What can I do? What do I want to learn to do?
Tornado	Violent force of destruction.	What dramatic change can I see approaching?

Torture	Part of the self tormented by the rest.	How am I hard on myself?
Toy animal	Playful relationship with the natural world. Freedom from responsibility.	Where do I want more pleasure in my life?
Toys	Youthful play. Practicing life's responsibilities.	In what way am I ready to enjoy my life more?
Train *See also* Travel; Vehicles.	Movement made while observing the areas covered or traveled.	What do I wish to observe as I change my life?
Trance *See also* Channeling.	Altered state. Expanded consciousness.	What part of my inner self am I ready to explore?
Travel *See also* Vehicles.	Movement from one way of life or attitude to another.	Where am I going? Where do I want to go?
Treasure	Fulfillment. Integration. Material or spiritual reward.	What do I need to feel complete?

Image:	Associations:	Ask Yourself:
Treaty *See* Agreement.		
Tree	Natural process. Structure of life.	Where in my life am I ready to grow?
Trial	Test. Resolution of conflict.	What is at issue?
Triangle *See also* Three.	Dynamic power. Integration of opposites.	Where in my life am I developing power by integrating internal opposition?
Tricycle *See also* Vehicles.	Immature power. Playful movement.	Am I mature enough to get there? Am I enjoying the journey?
Trousers *See also* Clothing.	Lower self. Passions.	What signals am I sending?

Truck *See also* Vehicles.	Ability to carry the load.	Can I handle the responsibility?
Tumor	Protective growth.	What old pain am I ready to release?
Tunnel	Path through inner space. Ordeal.	What light leads me on?
Turd *See* Excrement.		
Turquoise *See also* Colors.	Healing. Good luck. Protection.	Where in my life do I feel safe?
Turtle *See also* Animals, wild.	Protection. Perseverance.	Where in my life do I feel safe when I take my time?
Twenty-two *See also* Numbers.	Earthly mission. Self and others.	What do I trust?

Image:	Associations:	Ask Yourself:
Two *See also* Numbers.	Duality. Opposition. Balance. Partnership.	How do I relate?
UFO *See also* Alien.	Fear and joy of the unknown. Distant realms.	Where am I ready to expand into unknown realms?
Umbilical cord	Link between old and new self.	How am I connected with my emerging self?
Underground	Unconscious material.	What is ready to rise to consciousness?
Underpants *See* Clothing; Underwear.		

Term	Meaning	Question
Underwater *See also* Swimming; Water.	Submersion in emotion.	What emotions am I submerged within?
Underwear *See also* Clothing.	Private self. Sexual identity.	What are my hidden feelings?
Undressing	Exposing true or inner self.	Who am I underneath it all?
Unicorn	Purity. Magical consciousness. Union of divine and animal nature.	Where in my life am I ready to align my animal nature with my spiritual essence?
Uniform *See also* Clothing.	Conformity.	Where in my life do I wish to share with others or to break free of rules?

Image:	Associations:	Ask Yourself:
Universe	Totality of being. Wholeness.	Where in my life do I feel complete?
Urinating *or* urine *See also* Bathroom.	Release, usually of emotion. Anger. Embarrassment at emotional release.	What feelings am I clearing? Am I pissed off?
Vaccination	Protective injection.	What am I afraid of catching?
Vagina *See also* Body parts.	Feminine sexuality. Yin receptivity.	What do I receive? What receives me?
Valley	Protection. Safety. Ease.	What makes me comfortable?

Vampire	Energy-draining fear.	What pursues me? Where in my life do I deny my own power?
Vegetable	Healthy food. Natural sustenance.	What am I hungry for?
Vehicles *See also subheadings.*	Power. Movement. What gets you there.	How powerful am I? How do I feel about power?
—bicycle	Self-propulsion. Recreation.	Do I have enough strength to make it? Will it be fun?
—boat	Movement across the depths of feeling.	What emotions can I safely negotiate?
—brakes	Control or slowing of movement.	Where in my life am I ready to feel more secure with my power?

Image:	Associations:	Ask Yourself:
—*bus*	Shared journey. Mass transit.	How does my personal power relate to mass consciousness?
—*car*	Personal power. Ego.	Can I get there? Who am I?
—*convertible*	Glamourous power. Parade.	What power am I ready to display?
—*helicopter*	Movement in many directions.	Where in my life do I want more freedom of movement?
—*hydrofoil*	Soaring above the sea of feeling.	What emotions no longer inhibit me?
—*limousine*	Luxurious power. Extravagance.	Where in my life am I ready to be conspicuous in my expression of power?

—*motorcycle* Virility. Vigor. Display. How hot am I? Where in my life am I ready to be more masterful?

—*plane* Rapid movement across great distance. Am I in a hurry for change?

—*R.V.* The joy of power. Rugged amusement. Where in my life am I ready to have more fun with my power?

—*seat belt* Safety restraint. What holds my power in check?

—*tires* Cushion. Shock absorption. Where in my life do I need to smooth my way?

—*train* Movement made while observing the areas covered or traveled. What do I wish to observe as I change my life?

—*tricycle* Immature power. Playful movement. Am I mature enough to get there? Am I enjoying the journey?

Image:	Associations:	Ask Yourself:
—*truck*	Ability to carry the load.	Can I take on the responsibility?
Veteran	Survivor of conflict.	What battle is over for me?
Video games	High-tech competition. Skill. Dexterity.	What new abilities are available to me?
Violet *See also* Colors.	Spirituality. Boundary between visible and invisible realms. Aristocracy.	To what do I aspire?
Volcano	Eruption of unconscious or repressed material.	What must I clear?
Vomit *or* vomiting	Throwing up indigestible thoughts or feelings.	What do I need to get rid of?
Walking	Natural movement. Exercise.	Where am I going? Am I moving fast enough?

Wall	Barrier. Protection.	What is on the other side?
War	Violence. Conflict.	What parts of me are in conflict?
Warehouse	Storage of resources.	What am I ready to put away or to unpack?
Warrior *See* Soldier; Veteran; War.		
Wart	Noxious growth. Ugliness.	Where in my life am I ready to be more attractive?
Wasp	Stinging anger.	Where in my life do I want to strike out?
Water *See also* Elements.	Emotion. Dissolving. Yielding. Fluid. Release. Cleansing.	What am I feeling?

Image:	Associations:	Ask Yourself:
—creek	The flow of feeling.	What feelings flow comfortably within me?
—dripping	Trickle of emotion.	What am I releasing, bit by bit?
—flood	Overflow of emotion.	What feelings are too much for me?
—fountain	Emotion springing forth. Freedom of emotional expression. Release.	What feelings are welling up in me?
—frozen	Preservation. Restraint.	What rigid feelings am I ready to dissolve?
—harbor	Shelter. Safety.	Where in my life do I find emotional peace?
—ice	A rigid feeling state. Frozen.	What feelings are locked within or ready to be melted away?

—*lake*	Contained emotion. Often a sense of tranquility or peace.	What feelings do I comfortably contain?
—*mist*	Delicate expanse of feeling. Cool and comfortable.	What emotional field surrounds me?
—*ocean*	Vast, limitless feeling. Sometimes an overwhelming emotion. Rich with abundant life.	What part of me relates to such vastness?
—*rain*	Release of emotion. May be gentle and nourishing or dramatically threatening.	What feelings are pouring down on me?
—*river*	Flowing and active. May include dangerous rapids; may be smooth and tranquil.	What feelings are actively moving within me?
—*sea*		

See Water: *ocean.*

Image:	Associations:	Ask Yourself:
—spring	Source. Beginning.	Where in my life am I allowing my feelings new expression?
—stream See Water: creek.		
—swamp	Overwhelming, turgid feelings.	What old emotional patterns are beginning to change for me?
—swimming pool	The water of feeling contained by cultural constructs. Safety.	What feeling do I wish to safely contain?
—tidal wave	Overwhelming emotion.	What feelings are threatening to me?
—waterfall	Dramatic going with the flow. May be frightening or powerfully releasing.	Where in my life am I ready to take the plunge?

—well	Source. Shared resources.	What feelings am I ready to share?
Weapon	Work on expression of energy. Offense and defense. Aggression.	Where in my life am I ready to be more open and receptive?
Web	Network. Skill. Trap.	How do my abilities relate to each other? What holds me back?
Weed	Rugged fertility. Undesired growth.	What am I cultivating?
Well *See also* Water.	Source. Shared resources.	What feelings am I ready to share?
West	Ending. Death. Return to beginning.	Where am I heading?
Whale *See also* Animals, wild.	Power of the unconscious. Truth and strength of inner being.	What great truth am I ready to accept?

Image:	Associations:	Ask Yourself:
White *See also* Colors.	Purity. Clarity. Coldness.	What do I seek to purify?
Whore *See also* Prostitute.		
Widow *or* widower	Solitude. Isolation.	What part of me is lonely?
Wife	Yin aspect of self. Partner.	What have I joined with?
Wind *or* windy	Stimulation. Sensory overload.	Where in my life do I seek stimulation? Where do I feel overwhelmed?
Window *See also* House.	Vision. Seeing and being seen.	What am I willing to see? What do I wish to reveal or conceal?
Wing	Flight. Freedom. Transcendence.	What am I ready to rise above?

Winter	Cycle of disintegration. Rest. Rebirth.	What am I preparing to bring forth?
Witch	Negative feminine. Black magic. If positive, intuition and natural wisdom.	What feminine power do I hold or fear?
Wolf *See also* Animals, wild.	Instinct. Appetite. Threat. Loyalty.	What instincts are a threat to me? What are my instinctive loyalties?
Woman	Feminine aspect. Receptivity.	Where in my life am I ready to be more receptive?
Woods *See* Forest.		
Worm	Decay. Insignificance.	Where in my life am I ready to assert myself?
Wound *or* wounded	Site of grief or anguish.	What damage am I ready to heal?

Image:	Associations:	Ask Yourself:
Wreck	Violent destruction. Barrier to progress.	What or who wants to stop me?
Writing	Self-expression. Record of experience.	What do I wish to put on record?
X ray	Seeing inside. Dangerous energies.	What lies within? What do I fear if I penetrate the surface image?
Yard *See* Garden; Grass.		
Yellow *See also* Colors.	Vitality. Intellect. Clarity.	What do I wish to understand?
Yeti *See also* Animals, wild.	Man-beast. Legendary.	What part of my greater self is stalking me?

Young *or* **youth**   Immaturity. Vitality.   What part of me is blossoming?

Zoo   Wildness under control.   What instincts do I want to observe or enjoy in safety?
See also
Animals, wild.

Appendix
Additional Resources for Rewarding Dream Work

Beyond Your Wildest Dreams: Dream Incubation Tapes, Series I and II

Dream incubation tapes offer you an efficient, convenient means of intensifying and directing your dreams. You should use them at night, preferably with headphones, as you are falling to sleep.

Each tape begins with a guided meditation that relaxes your body and clears your mind, producing a body-relaxed, alert mind state similar to the state associated with various systems of meditation. The tapes then guide you to create intense images and visions that will lead to stimulating and memorable dreams.

The original music accompanying the tapes was produced for the series by the internationally acclaimed composer Deuter.

Following is a description of each of the tapes in Series I and II.

Series I

Tape 1

Side One: Dream Clearing. If you are interested in beginning a program of conscious dreaming, I recommend you start with this tape, which was created specifically to help you remove old dream material. Old images, and particularly recurrent dream patterns that may have been blocking your dream memory for years, will be processed and washed from your consciousness. Listen to "Dream Clearing" for a few nights before you turn the cassette over to Side Two and begin enjoying the delicious, sensuously rich dream experiences that the "Dream Recall" side often produces.

Side Two: Dream Recall. This tape stimulates each sense with vivid images. The result is intense dream imagery and better recall of it.

Tape 2

Side One: Dream Guidance. This tape leads to a dream meeting with the aspect of yourself that can guide you comfortably and securely into knowledge of your own future.

Side Two: Dream Healing. Through guided imagery, you visit Epidauros—healing center of the ancient world—to receive dreams that stimulate healing on an inner level.

Tape 3

Side One: Dream Exploration. Fly into dream adventures and explore other realms of consciousness while your body sleeps safely and comfortably.

Side Two: The Black Velvet Room. This tape opens a dream world of sensuous pleasure and deep, refreshing sleep—an antidote to even the most stressful waking life. A number of clients have reported to me that this tape is an effective antidote for insomnia.

Series II

Tape 1

Side One: Dreamsex. Explore the depths of your own sexuality in the privacy and safety of the dream state.

Opening the dream door to sexual fulfillment often leads to greater creative vitality in your waking life.

Side Two: The Corridor of Dreams. This tape encourages dreams that offer specific information about your future projects — including their most likely outcome and barriers to their success.

Tape 2

Side One: Dreamlover. This tape leads to a meeting in the dream state with your ideal other. You may meet an aspect of yourself, ready for integration, or actual future lovers, who invite you to approach them and complete the union so deeply desired.

Side Two: The Dark Vessel. This tape uses the classic imagery of setting out in a small boat across an expanse of dark water. I originally created it to lead the dreamer to the "other side" — to dream contact with friends and relatives who have passed away. It has also provided a valuable tool for a number of terminally ill clients who felt ready to explore the after-death state in their dreams. Because of the power of the imagery, "The Dark Vessel" also helps you investigate — and release — old fears and limitations. For several clients, it has worked well to alternate this tape with the "Dream Healing" tape (Series I, Tape 2, Side Two) or with the "Dream Clearing" tape (Series I, Tape 1, Side One).

I continue to use all of the tapes regularly, although I do have personal favorites and often choose "Dream Recall" (Series I, Tape 1, Side Two) simply because I love having all of my senses active in dreams — tasting dream food, smelling dream flowers, being acutely aware of colors and the texture of things.

I am presently working on a new series of tapes that invite greater input from the dreamer. If you are ordering tapes from either Series I or II, information on the new series will be included with your order.

For a full catalogue of tapes and information about dream workshops in your area, please write:

Real Dreams
P.O. Box 37520
Honolulu, HI 96837

Be sure to include your name, address, and phone number.

Invitation to Readers

Below is a space for you to jot down images that you did not find listed in Part Two and would like to see included in a future edition of *Understand Your Dreams*. We would be delighted to receive your comments and recommendations. Please mail your comments to:

Real Dreams
P.O. Box 37520
Honolulu, HI 96837

Order Form

Individual tapes are $10.00, plus $2.00 postage and handling. All three tapes of Series I can be ordered for $25.00 plus $3.50 postage and handling. Both tapes of Series II are $20.00 plus $2.50 postage and handling. (For delivery to areas outside the U.S., please add an additional $2.00 per order) Orders are payable in personal check or money order in U.S. funds. For Visa or Mastercard, please include the information requested below.

Please send me:

Series No.	Item Description:	Price Each	Total Cost
Series I	All three tapes of Series I	$28.50	$_____
Series I	Dream Clearing/Dream Recall	$12.00	_____
Series I	Dream Guidance/Dream Healing	$12.00	_____
Series I	Dream Exploration/The Black Velvet Room	$12.00	_____
Series II	Both tapes of Series II	$22.50	_____
Series II	Dreamsex/The Corridor of Dreams	$12.00	_____
Series II	Dreamlover/The Dark Vessel	$12.00	_____

Enclosed payment of: $_____

Make check or money order payable to:
Real Dreams, P.O. Box 37520, Honolulu, HI 96837
Method of payment: ☐check ☐money order ☐Visa ☐Mastercard

Credit Card Account Number: Expiration: Month   Year

☐☐☐☐☐☐☐☐☐☐☐☐☐☐☐☐   ☐☐   ☐☐

Credit card orders must include a signature.

Signature:_____Date:_____

Name:_____(please print)

Address:_____

City:_____ State:_____ Zip:_____

COMPATIBLE BOOKS FROM

H J KRAMER INC

WAY OF THE PEACEFUL WARRIOR
by Dan Millman
A tale of transformation and adventure . . . a worldwide best-seller.

SACRED JOURNEY OF THE PEACEFUL WARRIOR
by Dan Millman
"After you've read Sacred Journey *you will know
what possibilities await you."—WHOLE LIFE TIMES*

NO ORDINARY MOMENTS
by Dan Millman
*Based on the premise that we can change our world by changing ourselves,
Dan shares an approach to life that turns obstacles into opportunities,
and experiences into wisdom.*

THE LIFE YOU WERE BORN TO LIVE: FINDING YOUR LIFE PURPOSE
by Dan Millman
*Dan introduces a modern method based on ancient wisdom to help you
understand your past, clarify your present, and change your future.*

MESSENGERS OF LIGHT: THE ANGELS' GUIDE TO SPIRITUAL GROWTH
by Terry Lynn Taylor
At last, a practical way to connect with the angels and to bring heaven into your life!

GUARDIANS OF HOPE: THE ANGELS' GUIDE TO PERSONAL GROWTH
by Terry Lynn Taylor
*More than sixty practical angel practices that lead to more joy, hope, fun,
love and adventure in everyday life.*

ANSWERS FROM THE ANGELS: A BOOK OF ANGEL LETTERS
by Terry Lynn Taylor
*Terry shares the letters she has received from people all over the world,
telling of their experiences with angels.*

TALKING WITH NATURE
by Michael J. Roads
"From Australia comes a major new writer . . . a magnificent book!"
—RICHARD BACH, AUTHOR, *JONATHAN LIVINGSTON SEAGULL*

JOURNEY INTO NATURE
by Michael J. Roads
"If you only read one book this year, make that book
Journey Into Nature.*"—FRIEND'S REVIEW*

COMPATIBLE BOOKS FROM

H J KRAMER INC

THE EARTH LIFE SERIES
by Sanaya Roman
A course in learning to live with joy, sense energy, and grow spiritually.

LIVING WITH JOY, BOOK I
*"I like this book because it describes the way I feel
about so many things."*—VIRGINIA SATIR

PERSONAL POWER THROUGH AWARENESS: A GUIDEBOOK
FOR SENSITIVE PEOPLE, BOOK II
"Every sentence contains a pearl ..."—LILIAS FOLAN

SPIRITUAL GROWTH: BEING YOUR HIGHER SELF, BOOK III
*Orin teaches how to reach upward to align with the higher energies of the universe,
look inward to expand awareness, and move outward in world service.*

An Orin/DaBen Book
CREATING MONEY
by Sanaya Roman and Duane Packer, Ph.D.
This best-selling book teaches advanced manifesting techniques.

IN SEARCH OF BALANCE
by John Robbins and Ann Mortifee
*An inquiry into issues and concerns of the heart from the bestselling
author of* Diet for a New America.

THE COMPLETE HOME GUIDE TO AROMATHERAPY
by Erich Keller
*An easy-to-use guide to aromatherapy that opens the door to
the magical world of natural scents.*

YOU THE HEALER: THE WORLD-FAMOUS SILVA METHOD ON
HOW TO HEAL YOURSELF AND OTHERS
by José Silva and Robert B. Stone
You the Healer *is the complete course in the Silva Method healing techniques
presented in a do-it-yourself forty-day format.*

THE WIZDOM WITHIN
by Susan Jean and Dr. Irving Oyle
*"Fascinating! Illuminating. . . Reading this book can be hazardous to your
preconceptions."*—WILLIS HARMON, PRESIDENT, INSTITUTE OF NOETIC SCIENCES